S.O.S.

SIN Or

SICKNESS

You Must Decide

by

Dr. Stan K. McCrary

ISBN: 978-0-9842649-9-5

SOS, Sin or Sickness, You Must Decide is published by Oakes Books, oneoakes@gmail.com. Copyright © 2021 by Oakes Books, Seattle Washingtton, 98144. Printed and distributed in the United States by Lightning Source, Scriptures taken from King James, Online NKJV. Lessons and/or studies based on Dr. Stan K McCrary research analysis.

FOREWORD

This book is the examination of the Spiritual and Psychological impact of calling sin a disease. In the field of Biblical Counseling, there exists a significant quandary for Church members who want a biblical answer to their problems. This quandary is due to the Church incorporating psychological solutions in addition to biblical ones.

Several questions need addressing:

1. How did counselors in the Church adopt secular psychological concepts?
2. How has that adoption affected counseling ministries in the Church?
3. What is the appeal of using the vocabulary of Humanistic Psychology?

The answers to these and other similar questions are in a survey administered to several local pastors and Christian Counselors. Their answers are to analyze, interpret, and debate the various psychological and clinical words and phrases used to redefine sin. The survey will focus on three infamous "sicknesses," which are in the Bible as "sin." They are Alcoholism, Sexual Addiction, and Bipolar Disorder. All the surveys will convey the percentage of participants who identify these three diseases as Sin or Sickness and why.

The information obtained from this study will allow counselors and counseling ministries in the Church to define sinful and deviant behavior as "sin correctly" and not label it as "sickness" and to treat it accordingly.

Sin or Sickness

You Must Decide

Table of Contents

CHAPTER ONE

INTRODUCTION

Background

A war between the Church and the World started in the Garden of Eden. This war is about words. This war contains many battles which are having a devastating effect on the Church. The most decisive battle is using the words "Sin" and "Sickness." This battle is taking place in the field of Counseling.

The field of Counseling is in three types of practice:

1. Secular Counseling – According to Hector Chavez, "Secular Counseling is grounded in Humanism and most often seeks to help a person adjust to difficult circumstances. The processes may include client education, behavioral techniques, and cognitive restructuring (changing one's thoughts), just to name a few. However, the end goal will most likely be some adaptation that provides symptom relief. In Secular Counseling, the problem or the client often remains the focus (Chavez, 2020)."

2. Christian Counseling – "A practice that combines the counselor's faith and the principles of psychology to improve the counselee's mental health (Langham, 2020)."

3. Biblical Counseling – "a Biblical Counseling methodology grounded in the conviction that Holy Scriptures being God's law and testimony is true and should serve as our standard for all matters of faith and practice (Mack, 25)."

The Study

While studying as a Biblical Counseling student pursuing a doctorate in Biblical Counseling from Masters International School of Divinity, I was given an assignment by my instructor, Dr. David Tyler. In his class, Advanced Essentials in Biblical Counseling, he assigned me to find 20 sins that are now called sicknesses. I found 25 and I'm convinced that there are more.

This revelation has led me to believe that the Church has lost its identity, its purpose. The Church is more than just a gathering of baptized believers. The Church's purpose is in Acts 2.42: "*They devoted themselves to the apostles' teaching and to the fellowship, to the breaking of bread and to prayer.*" According to this verse, the Church's purposes should be:

1. Teaching Biblical Doctrine,
2. Providing a place of Fellowship for Believers,
3. Observing the Lord's Supper, and
4. Praying.

At the very beginning, it says, "the Apostles' teaching." The apostles taught that sin is purposely disobeying the rules of God (I John 3.4,). The apostles taught that the Church is not to be like the World (Rom.12.2). Sadly, the Church has allowed secular words to twist and distort their true spiritual meaning. The Bible teaches that the causes of tribulations, troubles, struggles, and sweats that result in harmful, unhealthy, damaging feelings are Depression, Anxiety, Fear and Disease.

These causes are organic, demonic possession, and sin. For example, Jesus heals a man and says to him,

> "*Behold, thou art made whole: sin no more, lest a worse thing come unto thee.*" (John 5.14).

This man, now healed, is warned by Jesus not to continue in his sin otherwise a worse condition may come upon him. His infirmity of 38 years was caused by his sins. Another example is found in 1 Cor.11. The members of the Church in Corinth were abusing the Lord's Supper. They had failed to "examine themselves" (v28) and were not worthy to have partaken in the Lord's Supper (v29). Their judgment comes in v30,

> "*For this cause many are weak and sickly among you, and many sleep.*"

If an organic cause cannot be found, then the root cause can be traced to the individual's behavior (or someone else's sinful behavior against them, as in child abuse). Therefore, there can be no other cause that can be categorized as "mental illness." Ungodliness is man's attitude towards God. Unrighteousness is man's attitude towards his fellow man. The consequence of ungodliness is unrighteousness. The consequence of unrighteousness is terrible feelings. Therefore, ungodliness leads to unrighteousness, which leads to:

- Guilt (Heb.10.2, 22),
- Depression (Matt.11.28, 1 Peter 5.7),
- Anxiety (Phil. 4.6, John 14.1-4),
- Shame (Ps. 31.17, 1 John 1:9),
- Fear (2 Tim. 1.7, 1 John 4.18), etc.

Behavior affects the way a person feels. Bad behavior stimulates bad feelings to warn us that we have violated God's rules and standards. This information was a revelation.

3

Many people in the Church believe they are "sick," that they have a "disease" when they are suffering from unrepentant sin.

1. How did this deception come about?
2. How and when did it enter the Church?

The purpose of this book is to inform pastors of the danger of confusion that exists when they send their congregants to psychologically trained individuals. The confusion is whom to believe, the Bible or the Diagnostic and Statistics Manual (DSM)?

Significance

One of the Biblical Counseling trends is the comprehensive examination of the creation, the fall, and man's redemption. To the Biblical Counselor, all sickness has its beginning in Adam's sin. However, psychology has spread like wildfire across America. Psychology is in the workplace, schools, homes, and even the Church. There is hope. Biblical Counselors will be able to use the current information in this study to readily combat the false propaganda the secular psychological community is feeding the public (especially the Church) concerning these "diseases" and show them that they are indeed curable through the power of God. Biblical Counselors will thereby be able to say that they use "Ratione Et Via Certus." Translation: "The method which is infallible" (Frey iii).

Conceptual Framework

This research will focus on three sins that are chronic or incurable in the DSM. These infamous "diseases" are Alcoholism, Stealing, and Bipolar Disorder.

Alcoholism

Alcohol Use Disorder (AUD, DSM-5 303.90 (F10.20))

Alcoholism is a combination of alcohol-related medical conditions characterized by alcohol dependence or alcohol abuse." (American Psychiatric Association, 2013, DSM 5th Edition). It is also more commonly referred to as alcoholism. According to the DSM-5e, AUD symptoms include craving, physical dependence, increasing tolerance for alcohol, .and loss of control. The DSM-5 does not offer a treatment plan for Alcohol Abuse Disorder but provides an excellent framework for diagnosing the illness. As with many psychological afflictions, there is no known cure for alcohol use disorder. In other words, there is no cure for alcoholism.

Stealing/Theft

Kleptomania (DSM-5 302.32 F63.3)

The DSM-5 criteria for stealing/theft calls for a diagnosis of Kleptomania (DSM-5 302.32 F63.3) include Recurrent impulses to steal—and instances of stealing—objects not needed for personal use or financial gain. According to the Mayo Clinic (mayo, 2020), "Kleptomania is difficult to overcome on your own. Without treatment, kleptomania will likely be an ongoing, long-term condition. However, there is no standard kleptomania treatment, and researchers are still trying to understand what may work best. It is not unusual to have relapses of kleptomania. To help avoid relapses, be sure to stick to your treatment plan. If you feel an urge to steal, contact your mental health professional or reach out to a trusted person or support group."

Bipolar Disorder

Bipolar I (DSM-5 296.40-296.50 F11-114

According to the American Psychiatric Association's Diagnostic and Statistical Manual of Mental Disorders (DSM-5), bipolar disorders are a group of brain disorders that cause extreme fluctuation in a person's mood, energy, and ability to function. Bipolar disorder is a category that includes three different conditions:

1. Bipolar I (DSM-5 296.40-296.50 F11-114), manic episodes that last at least seven days, or manic symptoms that are so severe that the person needs immediate hospital care,
2. Bipolar II (DSM-5 296.89 F31.81), one depressive episode lasting at least two weeks and at least one hypomanic episode lasting at least four days and
3. Cyclothymic Disorder (DSM-5 301.13 F34.0), a mood disorder that causes emotional highs and lows.

*Note that all three definitions are secular and not according to the Bible.

Methodology

The research solicited several Counselors, Christian Counselors, and local Pastors and through analytical examination, the survey contains questions that will attempt to reveal the following:

1. Their chosen method of counseling.
2. Their years of experience.
3. Their counseling credentials.
4. Do they feel their credentials are adequate for their diagnosis?

5. The foundation of their Counseling is based.
6. What are their opinions of the other two counseling methods?
7. Are they open to the other two counseling methods?
8. What is the counselor's definition of "Sin" and "Sickness?"
9. The counselor's definition of Alcoholism, Kleptomania, and Bipolar Disorder.
10. Does the Counselor classify Alcoholism, Kleptomania, and Bipolar Disorder as sickness or as a sin and why?

From a pool of over 60 hundred local Churches and two Counselors/Counseling Centers, five randomly selected Counselors and 15 Pastors were sent a survey and had two weeks to complete and return.

Their answers are to analyze, interpret, and debate the various psychological and clinical words and phrases used to redefine sin.

- This study is partial to using the Qualitative Research Method because there is a need to be more exploratory considering the current world affairs, however; the use of interviews and case studies would be more conducive. Conversely, there will be a need to incorporate some Quantitative Research degree. Therefore, we will depict multiple variables and seeks to determine a relationship between these variables using numbers, surveys, and charts. In conclusion, based on these variables we are inclined to use the quantitative method in the furtherance of his book. Also, Statistical data from peer articles and journals were used.

CHAPTER TWO

THE POWER OF WORDS

LITERATURE SURVEY

A New Vocabulary

In his 1839 play, Cardinal Richelieu, novelist and playwright Edward Bulwer-Lytton wrote the words, "*The pen is mightier than the sword.*" His main character, Cardinal Richelieu, was indicating that the written word is long-lasting and more powerful than the sword, which represents short-lived violence (Bulwer-Lytton, Cardinal Richelieu, Act II, Scene II).

Words! Words are powerful. Words can inspire and comfort. Words can move us to act. Words can calm a restless mob and bring Peace to a troubled mind. Words affect our thoughts and our feelings. When we speak, we should speak with mindfulness to solidify Peace and Compassion in our characters.

Not only do our words matter, but also the tone which we use has a considerable impact. There are specific rules that should guide all our communications with others. Always speak the truth and avoid exaggerations. Be consistent in what one is saying, do not use double standards in addressing people. Please do not use one's words to manipulate others, and most importantly, do not use words to insult or belittle anyone. Change a word's usage, and one must be careful how and when one says it.

"Literally" used to mean something taken quite seriously and without hyperbole. Now, it means the same as "a lot" in many people's vocabulary (dictionary.com 2020). "I love you" used to mean something is vital and committed, maybe even eternal. Now, it describes the feeling of the hour. To be sure, language evolves, and the meanings of words change with context. We must understand the impact of words; words matter. Words are lovely and beautiful tools. It is a shame that out of ignorance, we so often abuse them.

In the mid-1960s, a noteworthy event occurred in the Church concerning the word "Sin." The Church stopped calling sinful and deviant behavior "sin" and started calling it "sickness" (Tyler, 2). This action is in the sins Paul describes. In 1 Cor. 6.10, the drunkard is now called an alcoholic; the thief is now a kleptomaniac. In Chapters 6-9, the sexual sinner is now called a sex addict. In 1 Tim. 5.8, the father who does not work is worse than an infidel. Prov. 14.1 says that the wife who does not keep her home pulls it down. Eph. 6.1-3 states that disobedient children shorten their lifespan because obedience brings long life. This family is no longer in sin; it is dysfunctional. The "deeds of the flesh" (sinful behaviors), recorded in Gal. 5.19-21, are redefined by the World and embraced by the Church. When sin is called sickness, salvation is no longer needed. The drunkard has a disease called alcoholism. He is no longer accountable for his behavior. He is "sick." Instead of needing to repent, he needs a twelve-step recovery program. Calling sin sickness changes the salvation equation. Sick people need recovery. Sinners need forgiveness from God.

Secular vs Spiritual – The Word War

Words are powerful. In Genesis Chapters 1-3, we read that God created everything with His Word. God reveals himself to man through His Word. In the Garden of Eden, Satan presented Adam and Eve with a different interpretation of God's Word. Sadly, they believed him instead of God.

Interpretation is explaining the meaning of something. We live in a world where there are many different interpretations of the same set of facts, or as some say, "Alternative Facts." For example, one person looks at a child's behavior and sees a chemical imbalance in the child's brain requiring medication. The child is "sick." Another person will look at the same child and see rebellion and "sin." What is the difference? It is not the fact (the child's behavior) but the interpretation of the fact (sickness vs sin) that is the real issue.

In Eph. 6.10-18, Paul describes the armor God has provided for us to wear as we engage in spiritual warfare. Our weapon is in v17b as the sword, the Word of God. This weapon can be both offensive and defensive. If God's Word is misinterpreted, the sword is neutralized, and the soldier, the Christian, has no offensive weapon. He can only be on the defensive, which is a losing strategy.

In the Nineteenth Century, humanity was formally introduced to Sigmund Freud's Worldview (Wood, 60). A worldview is a set of beliefs that shapes the way a person views their World. Freud pointed out that we have unconscious drives that can affect our actions without us knowing about them. His psychoanalysis involved studying the human mind to help people deal with neuroses or other sorts of problems. Freud found that people had often repressed certain events in their life—buried them deep in their unconscious—and that these events were the cause of their malaise. Freud felt that our minds contain three parts. The id is our desire for pleasure. The ego takes reality into account and regulates the id. Furthermore, the superego is the societal morality that regulates everything we do (sparknotes.com, 2020).

The World of human ideas changed immediately. Freud described his Worldview as secular and called it "scientific," He claimed that no source of knowledge of the universe exists other than "carefully scrutinized observation what we call research." Therefore, no knowledge, he said, can be derived from revelation or intuition. He would declare that if one observes human behavior, one will notice the primary purpose of life is to find happiness and to find pleasure. Thus, Freud devised the "Pleasure Principle" as one of our existence's main features (independence.org, 2020). Here is the irony: Freud, professing himself a scientist practicing the scientific method, plucked his thin air theories. He then set about using his considerable intelligence and powers of persuasion to increase their plausibility. Finally, he made them acceptable to his disciples.

Humanity has been at war with this Worldview since the Garden. Christians need to embrace a Christian worldview that is not a collection of bits and pieces from here and there but totally and initially designed by God.

The Church is replacing spiritual words, taught by the Spirit, with worldly words taught by human wisdom (the World). In 1 Cor. 2.3, the Apostle Paul condemns the mixing of Spiritual Words with Worldly words. He says,

> "Which things also we speak, not in the words which man's wisdom teaches, but which the Holy Ghost teaches; comparing spiritual things with spiritual."

Paul says that we should not exchange God's words, which are real, with human words, misleading. For example, the human word "alcoholic" is not in the Bible, but the "drunkard" is the Spiritual word. It defines a person who habitually gets intoxicated. The human word "kleptomaniac" is not in the Bible, but the Spiritual word "thief" is.   It defines a person who habitually steals. Note in both examples of the Spiritual definition; there is the word "habitually." The Bibles teach that these two sins, "drunkard" and "thief," are habits that the person has formed by their choices.

The Church should use Spiritual words taught by the Spirit to portray God's reality accurately.   Once again, Paul advises the Church. In Col. 2.8, he says,

> *"Beware lest any man spoil you through philosophy and vain deceit, after the tradition of men, after the rudiments of the world, and not after Christ."*

In this context, Paul is condemning philosophy based on explicitly anti-Christian principles. Sadly, the Church has not listened to Paul. The Church no longer listens to the Word of God. Instead, the Church is accepting the wisdom of the World. Thus, the war continues.

The Words that We Use ...

Proverbs 18.20-21(KJV):

"20 A man's belly shall be satisfied with the fruit of his mouth; and with the increase of his lips shall he be filled.

21 Death and life are in the power of the tongue: and they that love it shall eat the fruit thereof."

Proverbs 18.20-21(Amp):

"20 A man's moral self shall be filled with the fruit of his mouth, and with the consequence of his words he must be satisfied (whether good or evil).

21 Death and life are in the power of the tongue, and they who indulge it shall eat the fruit of it (for death or life)."

The book of Proverbs is filled with much wisdom and these verses tell us of the power of our words. Most people do not realize that the things they speak, positive or negative, will affect their lives. We all have known people who are habitual complainers. They are always confessing a scenario of bad things that could happen. Many of these scenarios do happen to them, because they are not walking in faith. On the other hand, people who voice a positive confession of faith in the face of their troubles, are an inspiration to others and many are granted miracles to overcome the obstacles in their lives.

We must learn to set a guard on our mouths, as it is very important to control our conversation. We will ultimately receive the things that we speak. If we speak evil long enough, it will come to pass;

14

likewise, if we speak good. We must also realize that we shall be judged for the things we speak. In fact, the Bible tells us that the things that come out of our mouths actually reveal the things that are in our hearts. We all occasionally speak things that we should not speak; however, the things that we speak in abundance are the things in our hearts. The things we embrace in our hearts will bear fruit. We will reap what we sow with our words, as well as our deeds.

> *Matthew 12.33-37*
>
> *"33 Either make the tree good, and his fruit good; or else make the tree corrupt, and his fruit corrupt: for the tree is known by his fruit.*
>
> *34 O generation of vipers, how can ye, being evil, speak good things? for out of the abundance of the heart the mouth speaketh.*
>
> *35 A good man out of the good treasure of the heart bringeth forth good things: and an evil man out of the evil treasure bringeth forth evil things.*
>
> *36 But I say unto you, That every idle word that men shall speak, they shall give account thereof in the day of judgment.*
>
> *37 For by thy words thou shalt be justified, and by thy words thou shalt be condemned."*

Proverbs 18.21 tells us that death and life are in the power of the tongue. There is a principle of death and life that exists in the world. Certain things bring life, while others produce death. An example would be if we do not care for our physical bodies properly, eventually sickness will attack us that can lead to death. On the other hand, eating properly and exercising, etc. bring life and strength to our bodies.

In like manner, the words we speak will bring life to us, or death. There is another scripture in Proverbs that verifies this.

> *Proverbs 17.22:*
> *"A merry heart doeth good like a medicine: but a broken spirit drieth the bones."*

For someone to have a merry heart, they will certainly be cheerful in their talk. We can choose to speak good and cheerful things, or we can choose to voice negative things. We have a term for those who complain all the time. We say they are "down in the mouth." We can overcome our problems by speaking the Word of God over them. When I feel weak or tired, I quote this scripture:

> *Ephesians 6.10:*
> *"Finally, my brethren, be strong in the Lord, and in the power of his might."*

I thank God that I am strong in the Lord and the power of His might. I do not have to rely on my own strength, but rather, the strength of the Lord. When I voice this scripture as a prayer, soon I actually am stronger and feel better. However, the opposite will work against me if I start complaining how bad I feel and how weak I feel. While the feelings may be real, the Word of God is greater than my feelings and as I confess it over my problem, soon I feel better. Truly, life and death are in the power of the tongue.

> *Psalm 19.14:*
> *"Let the words of my mouth, and the meditation of my heart, be acceptable in thy sight, O LORD, my strength, and my redeemer."*

Amen.

The Church MUST Decide!

The Church is at a crossroads. It must decide whom it is going to believe. Due to following, the World's wisdom; the Church is in trouble. Today's theology is a hybrid blend of two antithetical worldviews. What is popular and psychological eclipses what is theologically sound Theologically. It is rooted in atheistic Darwinism, the biblical model replaced by the therapeutic leaves no space for man, that is created in the image and likeness of his Creator.

There was a time when the Church, facing problems, would seek God. Today, when faced with the same problems, the Church seeks a therapist. In Rom. 1.18, the Apostle Paul once again provides guidance that the Church has forgotten. He says,

> *"For the wrath of God is revealed from heaven against all ungodliness and unrighteousness of men, who hold the truth in unrighteousness."*

Paul abruptly transitions to the truth of the divine anger upon unrepentant sinners. Having laid out the good news in v1-17, he now gives the bad news. Here begins the case made for the need for the Gospel. These verses could be considered an answer to the questions, "

1. Why is the Gospel such a big deal?
2. Why do human beings need to be declared righteous by God?
3. What do we need to be saved from?

Notice how Paul lists ungodliness before unrighteousness. A person without God will not be righteous! As stated earlier, ungodliness is man's attitude towards God. Unrighteousness is a man's attitude towards his fellow man.

Paul continues with v19-23

Romans 1.19-23

19 Because that which may be known of God is manifest in them; for God hath shewed it unto them.

20 For the invisible things of him from the creation of the world are clearly seen, being understood by the things that are made, even his eternal power and Godhead; so that they are without excuse:

21 Because that, when they knew God, they glorified him not as God, neither were thankful; but became vain in their imaginations, and their foolish heart was darkened.

22 Professing themselves to be wise, they became fools,

23 And changed the glory of the uncorruptible God into an image made like to corruptible man, and to birds, and forefooted beasts, and creeping things.

These verses illustrate man's decision to become ungodly which then flows into unrighteousness. Therefore, the consequence of ungodliness is unrighteousness. Observe!

24 Wherefore God also gave them up to uncleanness through the lusts of their own hearts, to dishonour their own bodies between themselves:

25 Who changed the truth of God into a lie, and worshipped and served the creature more than the Creator, who is blessed forever. Amen.

26 For this cause God gave them up unto vile affections: for even their women did change the natural use into that which is against nature:

27 And likewise also the men, leaving the natural use of the woman, burned in their lust one toward another; men with men working that which is unseemly, and receiving in themselves that recompence of their error which was meet.

28 And even as they did not like to retain God in their knowledge, God gave them over to a reprobate mind, to do those things which are not convenient;

29 Being filled with all unrighteousness, fornication, wickedness, covetousness, maliciousness; full of envy, murder, debate, deceit, malignity; whisperers,

30 Backbiters, haters of God, despiteful, proud, boasters, inventors of evil things, disobedient to parents,

31 Without understanding, covenantbreakers, without natural affection, implacable, unmerciful:

32 Who knowing the judgment of God, that they which commit such things are worthy of death, not only do the same, but have pleasure in them that do them. "

Rom, 1.18–32 describes why God rightfully condemns humanity and some of what He has done about it. Humanity's fall is a downward progression.

It starts with rejecting God as Creator, refusing to see what is known about Him by what He has made. We also reject that He is our provider and stop giving Him thanks. We worship His creation instead of Him.

Finally, God acts by giving us over to the unchecked expression of our corrupt sexual desires and all other kinds of sin. In part, He expresses His wrath by giving us what we want and condemning us to suffer the painful consequences.

19

The Church is facing a society that has adopted a psychological worldview. God is no longer supreme and all-powerful. The Psychological Worldview has taken the World (and almost the Church) by storm. It is in the home, the schools, the workplace, the legal/judicial system, and even politics.

What about the Church? Many Churches today have incorporated some elements of psychological ideology. This ideology is dangerous! Why? Because the root of psychology is terrible, and therefore, the fruit cannot be right. Churches are hiring counselors as staff members to assist the congregation with mental issues.

This method is not the approach Jesus took. He met the needs, all the needs of the people through the power of the Holy Spirit, and the research of this book indicates He intends His Church to do the same. The Church do not have to depart and go to the World to get their emotional needs met. They should bring them to Jesus (Matt. 14.16-18). In this example, Jesus met the need and fed the multitude. As He met their need, He will meet the need of His Church.

> *Matthew 14.16-18*
>
> *16 But Jesus said unto them, They need not depart; give ye them to eat.*
>
> *17 And they say unto him, We have here but five loaves, and two fishes.*
>
> *18 He said, Bring them hither to me.*

The psychological Worldview advances the idea that everyone benefits from therapy and the goal of therapy is individual freedom. If one is "sick," you are not responsible for your actions. All one must do is follow the directions/orders of the therapist. It is the therapist who can "see" into your problem and prescribe a remedy. It is the counselor who is qualified and certified to help us. We must follow them without question. We need a therapist, not a Savior.

When did this happen? In the mid-1960s, the highways of therapeutic and Christian practices began to merge. This tangled mess has gripped the Church ever since. The Church has accepted the Worldview created by atheists. Just look at the traditionally Christian publishing companies that print articles and books based on anti-Christian theories. Evangelicals, those who belong to a worldwide trans-denominational movement within Protestant Christianity and maintain the belief that the essence of the Gospel consists of the doctrine of salvation by grace alone, solely through faith in Jesus's atonement, are in fact, promoting psychology.

Churches, Bible colleges and Seminaries, Christian speakers, and Christian publishers worldwide promote mental health programs to help Christians solve their problems and find personal fulfillment.

Many Christian educational institutions have added psychology classes and majors, and some include master's degree and Ph.D. programs in Psychology. Denver Seminary, Talbot Seminary, Trinity Evangelical Divinity School, Liberty University, Moody Bible Institute, Fuller Theological Seminary, and a host of other Christian schools teach that Psychology and the Bible must merge into Counseling. The Church is to remain relevant to our contemporary culture. Dallas Seminary employs one of the nation's best-known Christian psychiatrists on its teaching faculty. Colorado Christian University offers a counseling degree built on the theories of a prominent Christian psychologist.

Churches have adapted Twelve-Step programs patterned after Alcoholics Anonymous (A.A.) to address almost any persistent personal problem, from obesity to "spiritual" addictions. Some Churches offer a personality evaluation with membership forms to ensure that new members have their emotional and mental health needs met in addition to their spiritual needs. There are even study Bibles designed especially for people "in recovery." Indeed, some Christians argue that the inclusion of psychological principles and teachings into a biblical counseling setting is the only way to provide competent mental health care to Christians.

At the same time, there are those Christians who reject entirely any psychological theories or therapies, denouncing psychology as a rival religion and substitute for the atoning and cleansing work of Christ. Authors such as Dave Hunt and Jay Adams demarcate between "the psychological way" and "the spiritual way." Some Christians not only condemn psychology as ungodly and reflective of fallen man but also warn of spiritual deception and demonic attack as possible consequences of involvement in "secular psychology."

Many Christians are not prepared to embrace either of the above points of view. They see the issues as much more complicated than total acceptance or total rejection. They have genuine concern about how best to resolve their problems, and problems for those they love, and to whom they minister. Decisions, decisions ... The Church must decide!

CHAPTER THREE

THE MANUFACTURING OF MADNESS

The Creation of Diseases

> "The term disease broadly refers to any condition that impairs the normal functioning of the body. For this reason, diseases are associated with dysfunction of the body's normal homeostatic processes ("Disease," 2020)."

We understand the world around us by our ability to identify and classify things. We group things based on what they have in common and/or not in common. We call this grouping classification the action or process of classifying something according to shared qualities or characteristics ("Classification," 2020). The usefulness of any classification method and its respective names depends on the fact that it includes some things and excludes others. This usefulness is what has happened in medicine and psychology for the past century.

What counts as a disease also changes over historical time, partly because of increasing health expectations, partly due to diagnostic ability changes, but mostly for a mixture of social and economic reasons. At first, there were clear and distinct maladies such as cancer, strokes, polio, and other injuries. In the 19th century, Rudolf Virchow declared that *"diseases have no independent or isolated existence; they are not autonomous organisms, not beings invading a body, nor parasites growing on it; they are only the manifestations of life processes under altered conditions"* (Kräupl, 11).

As time moved forward, behaviors such as drunkenness, gambling, rebelliousness, and countless others were added to this class. They were not added because they were discovered to be bodily diseases but because the disease criterion was changed (Tyler, 53). The Church has accepted the new criterion of classifying disease without question. Sin is now sickness.

So, what is a disease? People have no clear idea of what is and what is not a disease. To properly define the word, it must have a narrow and limited meaning between literal and metaphorical uses. For example, a virus can cause a disease, but a computer virus causes no physical harm. Typhoid fever is a disease, but spring fever and cabin fever are not.

If a person is to have the correct view of the Christian faith, he must understand the subject of sin. Without this understanding, words such as justification and sanctification are just "words." Without sin, they have no meaning. 1 Cor. 15.3 says, *"Christ died for our sins."* If sin has no meaning, then Christ's death was in vain. Sin is the core issue on which the Church speaks (ibid 57). Christians who embrace the Worldview of sin being a sickness become enslaved to sin. Churches now have Christians who are sick instead of sinful. Relief is in a pill instead of repentance.

The Birth of Mental Illness

Scientists studying the developmental roots of mental illness have zeroed in on a likely suspect: the body's stress response. When the body reacts to stressors, two systems kick into gear. The endocrine system produces stress hormones such as cortisol. Furthermore, the sympathetic nervous system churns out other stress-related hormones such as epinephrine and norepinephrine.

These hormones are responsible for the heart-pounding, sweaty-palms sensation known as the fight-or-flight response.

However, stress physiology encompasses much more than just stress hormones, says Thaddeus Pace, Ph.D., an assistant professor of psychiatry and behavioral sciences at Emory University School of Medicine. Stress also impacts immune function. *"A stressful event can have profound effects on the amount of activity that's going on in the inflammatory immune system,"* he says ("The Beginning of Mental Illness," 2020).

"Stress" is defined as

a: a) force exerted when one body or body part presses on, pulls on, pushes against, or tends to compress or twist another body or body part especially: the intensity of this mutual force commonly expressed in pounds per square inch.

b: the deformation caused in a body by such a force.

c: a physical, chemical, or emotional factor that causes bodily or mental tension and may be a factor in disease causation ("Stress," 2020).

What does the Bible say about stress? While "stress" is not explicitly mentioned in the Bible, Scripture does speak to things such as anxiety, worry, and trouble—things we often associate with stress—and gives us clear answers on how we should deal with them. There are many different stress types: financial, marital, emotional, medical, physical, and even spiritual. Everyone suffers from stress at one time or another. How we naturally deal with it depends in large part on who we are. For some, emotional stress causes physical illness. Others might become hyper-productive.

On the other hand, some people under stress shut down mentally and emotionally. Stress is a common human experience, particularly in a world where the demands for our time and attention seem to be unending. Our jobs, health, family, friends, and even ministry activities can overwhelm us. The ultimate solution to stress is to surrender our lives to God and seek His wisdom regarding priorities and His enabling us to do what He calls us.

The Bible provides scores of solutions to the things which cause stress. Such as in James.

> James 1.2-4,
> *"2 My brethren, count it all joy when ye fall into divers temptations; 3 Knowing this, that the trying of your faith worketh patience. 4 But let patience have her perfect work, that ye may be perfect and entire, wanting nothing."*

No matter the type of stress in our lives, the starting point for dealing with it is Jesus Christ. Jesus offers us great encouragement in John.

> John 14.1,
> *"Let not your hearts be troubled. Believe in God; believe also in me."*

We desperately need Jesus in our lives. We need Him because He is the only one who can give us the strength to cope with our lives' troubles. Believing in Him does not mean that we will have a trouble-free life or that we will not feel overcome by stress in our lives. It merely means that a life without Jesus Christ makes coping with stress an impossible and often debilitating task. Perhaps no passage in Scripture better captures how to handle stress than Philippians.

> Philippians 4.6-7:
> *"Do not be anxious about anything, but in everything by prayer and supplication with thanksgiving let your requests be made known to God. Moreover, the Peace of*

God, which surpasses all understanding, will guard your hearts and your minds in Christ Jesus".

The Lord tells us not to be anxious about anything but rather to turn everything over to Him in prayer. Lifting our burdens and concerns to a holy and righteous God will mitigate or eliminate the stress in our lives every day. Psalm 55:22 tells us to cast all our cares on Him because He will sustain us and never fail us.

Jesus Christ offers Peace if we come to Him with our worries and concerns. He says in John.

> John 14.27,
> *"Peace I leave with you; my Peace I give to you. Not as the World gives do I give to you. Let not your hearts be troubled, neither let them be afraid."*

Stress of all kinds is a natural part of life; how we deal with it is up to us. If we choose to try to do it on our own, we will not find lasting relief. The only way we can consistently and successfully deal with stress is with Jesus Christ.

First, we must believe in Him. Second, we need to trust Him and obey Him. We should trust Him to do what is right because His ways are always best for us. Disobedience and sin can produce stress and cut us off from the only means of Peace and Joy. By obeying His commandments, we reap the blessings of true contentment from a loving God. Finally, we need to seek His Peace daily by filling our minds with His Word, lifting all things to Him in prayer, and sitting at His feet in awe and reverence. Only by His grace, mercy, and love can the stress in our lives be managed. He always gives enough, so we need not be defeated by stress.

The Diagnostic and Statistical Manual of Mental Health Disorders (DSM)

As the Bible is the source of spiritual knowledge and information to the Pastor, so is the Diagnostic and Statistical Manual of Mental Health Disorders (DSM), the source of psychological knowledge and information to the secular mental health professional. The Church needs to know that its members are diagnosed as having an illness (by the Secular World) when the illness's root cause is sin.

The Diagnostic and Statistical Manual of Mental Disorders (DSM; latest edition: DSM-5, publ. 2013) is a publication by the American Psychiatric Association (APA) to classify mental disorders using a common language and standard criteria. It is used by clinicians, researchers, psychiatric drug regulation agencies, health insurance companies, pharmaceutical companies, the legal system, and policymakers.

The DSM evolved from systems for collecting census and psychiatric hospital statistics and a United States Army manual. Revisions since its first publication in 1952 have incrementally added to the total number of mental disorders while removing those no longer considered mental disorders.

Recent editions of the DSM have received praise for standardizing psychiatric diagnosis grounded in empirical evidence instead of the theory-bound nosology used in DSM-III. However, it has also generated controversy and criticism, including ongoing questions concerning the reliability and validity of many diagnoses, the use of arbitrary dividing lines between mental illness and "normality"; possible cultural biases; and the medicalization of human distress ("DSM," 2020).

The DSM covers all categories of mental health disorders for both adults and children. It contains descriptions, symptoms, and other criteria necessary for diagnosing mental health disorders. It also contains statistics concerning which gender is most affected by the illness, the typical age of onset, the effects of treatment, and standard treatment approaches.

Like other medical conditions, the government and many insurance carriers require a specific diagnosis to approve payment treatment. Therefore, in addition to being used for psychiatric diagnosis and treatment recommendations, mental health professionals also use the DSM to classify patients for billing purposes ("Diagnostic and Statistical Manual (DSM) Overview," 2020).

The premise of the DSM is:

> 1. The patient is assigned a code the corresponds to the "disease" they suffer.
>
> 2. Using the assigned code, the patient receives treatment.
>
> 3. Based on the treatment, the caregiver is financially reimbursed.

The DSM's primary purpose is to capture, in one volume, a standard set of definitions used to diagnose and categorize mental illnesses. Medical professionals, psychologists, counselors, occupational and rehabilitation therapists, and social workers use the DSM daily to diagnose and for bill guidance. The DSM has become a central element in the diagnosing of mental illnesses in the psychological community. It is taught in psychology and psychiatry textbooks as the gold standard in diagnosing mental disorders. Despite its popularity, the DSM is not perfect.

Real science contains a four-step process:

1. Observation

2. Data collection

3. Creation of hypothesis/theory

4. Testing of the hypothesis

The DSM does not have these steps. Paula Caplan, Ph.D. (Psychology), stated: *"As a former consultant to those who construct the World's most influential manual of alleged mental illnesses, the American Psychiatric Association's (APA) Diagnostic and Statistical Manual of Mental Disorders (DSM), I have had an insider's look at the process by which decisions about abnormality are made. As a longtime specialist in teaching and writing about monitoring the truly astonishing extent to which scientific methods and evidence are disregarded as the handbook is being developed and revised"* (Caplan, xv).

She says, *"The point is not that decisions about who is normal are riddled with personal biases and political considerations but rather that, by dint of a handful of influential professionals' efforts, those subjective determinants of diagnosis masquerade as solid science and truth"* (Caplan, xvi).

Since the Garden of Eden, man has continued to run and try to hide from God. He has continued shifting the blame for his behavior onto others and covered his sin, so no one will see how depraved he is. The DSM is the pinnacle of his effort to date. A collection of sins or sin-related behaviors have been composed into convenient lists, labeled as diseases, explained to the Church using fundamentally flawed research tied to unproven chemical imbalances.

Drugs that may alter these chemicals are not what God gave us for the atonement of our sins. He provided His only begotten Son for that purpose.

CHAPTER FOUR

TACKLING SIN-DISEASE

Secular Counseling

What does it mean to be Secular?

Its simplest definition is:

1 a) of or relating to the worldly or temporal b) not overtly or specifically religious c) not ecclesiastical or clerical.

2 a) not bound by monastic vows or rules; specifically of, relating to, or forming clergy, b) not belonging to a religious order or congregation ("Secular," 2020).

To be secular is to maintain a naturalistic worldview. This Worldview believes that anything is proportionate to the evidence available. It is about engaging in various worldly activities and identifying with or being a member of non-religious groupings or associations. To be secular does not mean that one lacks belief. Secular people believe in all sorts of things, — but none of them are beliefs in supernatural deities, creatures, or realms (Zuckerman, 2020).

History of Secular Counseling

The history of the counseling field, though relatively new, is rich. It is essential to note the influence of psychology's broad field, and though much of the history of each is unique; Counseling and psychology are branches of the same mental health tree. The counseling field developed from the guidance movement in response to the recognition of a need for mental health and guidance counseling for individuals facing developmental milestones ("History of Counseling," 2020).

History of Counseling Psychology

Counseling psychology emerged as an applied specialty within the American Psychological Association (APA) in the 1940s. It has been recognized as a specialty by the APA since 1946. This recognition was reaffirmed in 1998 when the APA initiated a new period of application for specialty recognition ("History of Counseling Psychology," 2020).

In Secular Counseling, the desired result relates to increasing a person's ability to function more effectively or become more emotionally stable ("What is Christian Counseling versus Secular Counseling?", 2020). Secular Counseling does not offer any religious bias. A secular counselor may use a client's religion as a talking point but should not promote religious beliefs or shame the client for having a belief. A traditional therapist will look at one's relationship and find the causes be it unconscious thoughts, past trauma, or communication issues.

For secular Counseling, there is more concentration on the individual. While many problems have similar roots, each situation is a bit different, and the counselor will have to try many different techniques to find the solution that best fits them ("What Are The Differences Between Christian Counseling And Secular Counseling?", 2020).

What is wrong with Secular Counseling?

Secular Counseling's problem is its philosophy:

1. It is man solving his problems, using his resources, and no outside help; God and the spiritual dimension of humans are not brought into the equation.
2. Secular Counseling depends on human reason and research to answer questions concerning human problems or their solutions. It assumes that there is no final answer to life or meaning to life.

Why isn't secular psychology enough?

William Kirk Kilpatrick, a professor of educational psychology at Boston College, answered this question. He replied, *"Why isn't secular psychology enough? It offers plausible explanations, useful insights, good techniques. It offers perfect pills. Nevertheless, it does not offer the one thing that people require most: a sense of meaning. Quite the contrary, we can even say that the psychological sciences tend to reduce meaning. One comes away from the psychology textbooks because though life now seems more explainable, it somehow seems less meaningful. Everything we thought was of value gets explained away. Symphonies and paintings turn out to be a sublimation of the sex drive or productions of the right brain hemisphere. Love turns out to be a matter of stimulus and response or a series of transactions conditioned by family patterns.*

We may be close to why the rise of psychology has not ushered in the reign of happiness. It might give us skills for living; psychology has never given a reason for living. It offers no vision."

Solomon said it best.

> Prov. 29.18
> *"Where there is no vision, the people perish: but he that keepeth the law, happy is he."*

Have you lost your mind?

Phil 2.5-11

"5 Let this mind be in you, which was also in Christ Jesus:

6 Who, being in the form of God, thought it not robbery to be equal with God:

7 But made himself of no reputation, and took upon him the form of a servant, and was made in the likeness of men:

8 And being found in fashion as a man, he humbled himself, and became obedient unto death, even the death of the cross.

9 Wherefore God also hath highly exalted him, and given him a name which is above every name:

10 That at the name of Jesus every knee should bow, of things in heaven, and things in earth, and things under the earth;

11 And that every tongue should confess that Jesus Christ is Lord, to the glory of God the Father."

Introduction

Have you ever reached a place in your life where you felt yourself losing it? I don't know about you, but sometimes I've felt that way.

Some of us know somebody who has indeed "lost it" and now they need professional help. We often hear of a horrible crime and the accused individual will plea "Temporary Insanity" as their defense. For a brief moment, they lost their mind.

Now, some people think that you have lost your mind by virtue of the fact that you are a Christian. They cannot believe that you go to church as much as you do. They cannot believe that you enjoy going to church. They cannot believe that you could give a tenth or more of your income to your local church when you could use it for a new car, or a nice vacation, or something you deserve to have. As a matter of fact, quite frankly, they think you have lost your mind, and maybe you have.

Paul tells us in 1 Corinthians:

> *1 Cor 1.18-25*
>
> *"18 For the preaching of the cross is to them that perish foolishness; but unto us which are saved it is the power of God.*
>
> *20 Where is the wise? where is the scribe? where is the disputer of this world? hath not God made foolish the wisdom of this world?*
>
> *21 For after that in the wisdom of God the world by wisdom knew not God, it pleased God by the foolishness of preaching to save them that believe.*

23 But we preach Christ crucified, unto the Jews a stumblingblock, and unto the Greeks foolishness;

25 Because the foolishness of God is wiser than men; and the weakness of God is stronger than men."

You see, in a spiritual sense, to be the kind of Christian that God wants you to be it is necessary for you to lose your mind. In the text of this lesson, Paul gives three things to the Philippian church that are still relevant to us today. He gives the command (v5), the catalog (v6-8), and the conclusion (v9-11).

I. THE COMMAND v5

"5 Let this mind be in you, which was also in Christ Jesus:"

This is not a suggestion. It is in the imperative form. It means, just do it. You and I are expected to develop the attitude and actions that Jesus had shown. By virtue of the word, Christian, meaning "Christ like," we are to be like Christ. To be called a Christian and act or live some other way is contrary to the definition of the word Christian.

Letting the mind of Christ be in us means that we are to think as Christ would think, resulting in behavior typical of Christ. If we have the mind of Christ, we are not going to act different than Christ would act. Jesus said in Matthew:

Matt 5.6,

"Blessed are they which do hunger and thirst after righteousness: for they shall be filled."

To have the mind of Christ you must have a hunger for Him! Do you have a hunger or a taste for righteousness? It's easy to find out. When you have a "Hunger" for something you need it to survive, you got to have it to live! A "Taste" for something comes

36

and goes at your whim. When you have a "Hunger" for righteousness you can't wait to come to church! You know you need Sunday School and Bible Study for your Spiritual growth. You got to be here because you know that when you come to hear the Word of God you will be blessed! When you have a Hunger for the Word of God you go to church every Sunday, 1st, 2nd, 3rd, 4th, and the even the 5th! If you have this Hunger Jesus Christ says you are blessed and that you shall be filled!

However, if you have a "Taste" for righteous you come to church whenever you feel like it. You don't come to Sunday School, it too early and you need that extra hour of sleep. When you have just a Taste for righteous you don't come to church functions, you don't support the district and you don't even think about going to anybody's church on the 5th Sunday! You just got a taste!

That's the command. Lose your mind and take on the mind of Christ. Think like Christ would think so you will do what Christ would do.

II. THE CATALOG v6-8

If we are commanded to take on the attitudes and actions of Christ, then how are we to act? What things should be commonplace in our lives so that we might possess the mind of Christ? Paul mentions some of them here. There is a catalog items that Paul shares with us to help us here. The mind or thinking of Christ would that of:

A. SELFLESSNESS v6,7

6 "Who, being in the form of God, thought it not robbery to be equal with God:"

Let no one doubt that Jesus was God. He was co-equal with the Father. How many times in the Bible are we told that Jesus was divine?

> *John 10.30, "I and my Father are one."*

> *John 1.1, "In the beginning was the Word, and the Word was with God, and the Word was God."*

> *John 1.14, "And the Word was made flesh, and dwelt among us, (and we beheld his glory, the glory as of the only begotten of the Father,) full of grace and truth."*

7 "But made himself of no reputation, and took upon him the form of a servant, and was made in the likeness of men:"

This is an interesting verse. Literally, it says that Christ "emptied Himself." This describes the action of Christ. Be careful here. Some say that Christ emptied Himself of His deity when He came earthward. But He did not. He emptied Himself of His divine privileges, but not of His divinity. He imposed upon Himself limitations so He could identify with mankind. He was then and always will be 100% God. He was then and always will be 100% man. He is the God-man!

The first attitude we are to develop if we would have the mind of Christ is the attitude of selflessness.

B. SUBMISSION v8

The second attitude in Paul's catalog is that of Submission.

8 "And being found in fashion as a man, he humbled himself, and became obedient unto death, even the death of the cross."

Besides submitting Himself to the worst demotion in history, Christ yielded Himself to ridicule, arrest, mockery, beatings, and

38

finally death on the cross. If you want to know how much Jesus loves you, look at the cross. He gave up His throne in Heaven to submit Himself to the most excruciating and dehumanizing form of human punishment. Why?

    1. For Love -

> *John 3.16, "For God so loved the world, that he gave his only begotten Son, that whosoever believeth in him should not perish, but have everlasting life."*

    2. For Loyalty -

> *Mt 26.39, "And he went a little further, and fell on his face, and prayed, saying, O my Father, if it be possible, let this cup pass from me: nevertheless not as I will, but as thou wilt."*

The first attitude we are to develop if we would have the mind of Christ is the attitude of selflessness. The second attitude in Paul's catalog is that of submission. And the third attitude is that of Sacrifice.

C. SACRIFICE v8

8 "And being found in fashion as a man, he humbled himself, and became obedient unto death, even the death of the cross."

III. THE CONCLUSION v9-11

The Command, The Catalog, and last, The Conclusion

A. EXALTED NAME v9

"9 Wherefore God also hath highly exalted him, and given him a name which is above every name:"

Though He was thus humbled, and appeared in the form of a servant, He is now raised up to the throne of glory, and to universal dominion. This exaltation is spoken of the Redeemer as He was, sustaining a divine and a human nature. If there was, as has been supposed, some obscuration or withdrawing of the symbols of His glory (Phil 2:7), when He became a man, then this refers to the restoration of that glory, and would seem to imply, also, that there was additional honor conferred on Him. There was all the augmented glory resulting from the work which He had performed in redeeming man.

B. EVENTUAL EVENT v10-11

"10 That at the name of Jesus every knee should bow, of things in heaven, and things in earth, and things under the earth;

11 And that every tongue should confess that Jesus Christ is Lord, to the glory of God the Father."

The knee should bow, or bend, in token of honor, or worship; that is, all people should adore Him. Everyone should acknowledge Him. On the duty and importance of confessing Christ as Lord. The word "Lord," here, is used in its primitive and proper sense, as denoting owner, ruler, sovereign. The meaning is, that all should acknowledge him as the universal sovereign.

Conclusion

Why should we 'Loose Our Minds' and take on the attitude and actions of Christ?

> TO BE THE KIND OF CHRISTIAN GOD WANTS US TO BE, WE MUST BE WILLING TO GIVE UP OUR ATTITUDES, ASPIRATIONS AND ACTIONS SO THAT CHRIST'S ATTITUDE, ASPIRATIONS AND ACTIONS WILL BECOME OUR OWN.
>
> TO DO THIS, WE MUST FIRST LOOSE OUR MINDS –
>
> SO THAT WE MAY OBTAIN THE MIND OF CHRIST!

That's why Jesus died for you, so that you may be empowered to have His mind! He now sits on the right-hand side of God our Father. One day He is coming back...will you be ready? Glory to God!!!

Amen

Christian Counseling

If Secular Counseling is "freezing cold," and Biblical Counseling is "boiling hot," then Christian Counseling is "horribly lukewarm." In Rev. 3.16, Jesus says to the Church at Laodicea, *"So then because thou art lukewarm, and neither cold nor hot, I will spue thee out of my mouth."*

Lukewarm is defined as:

> 1: moderately warm: tepid; a lukewarm bath; lukewarm coffee.

> 2: lacking conviction: half-hearted; gave them only lukewarm support; a lukewarm review; lukewarm applause ("Lukewarm," 2020).

Christian Counseling is lukewarm. While it has excellent intentions, it fails. Christian Counseling aims to help people regain a sense of hope for their life found in Jesus Christ. Christian Counseling believes that at the core of what they do is to help others achieve a better understanding of themselves and God, which is rooted in the Holy Spirit's conviction ("Christian Counseling," 2020). In Christian Counseling, the primary goal is to enable the person to heal, to interact with God effectively, and utilize their gift in the body of Christ.

Christian Counseling is distinct from Secular Counseling in that it explicitly incorporates the spiritual dimension, Biblical truths, and a seeking of God's will in an individual's life ("Christian Counseling vs. Secular Counseling," 2020).

History of Christian Counseling

Christian Counseling was born out of debates about the sufficiency of Scripture. The debate began in the late 1960s with the work of Jay Adams. By the time Adams began to write about Counseling, it had been over a century since a Christian had written a book explaining how to use the Bible as the source of wisdom to help people with their counseling-related problems.

By the middle of the twentieth century, most Christians did not believe that the Bible was a book that was pointedly relevant for the kinds of conversations that happen when counseling someone with challenging problems. Instead, mainline Protestant pastors began to mix their liberal theology with secular psychological principles to create what became known as "Clinical Pastoral Care" (known today as Clinical Pastoral Education or CPE). Later, so-called integrationists sought to do the same thing but replaced liberal theology with conservative theology.

The evangelical commitments of the integration movement were an improvement. It led to less optimism and naiveté concerning secular psychologists' worldview commitments, but the outcome was the same. Whether liberal or conservative, Christians continued to believe that the Christian counseling resources found in the Bible were weak, while secular resources for counseling found in the modern psychological corpus were substantial.

In the middle of the twentieth century, Christians were helping people with their problems. Their efforts become a conversation about how much and what kind of secular psychology adds to Scripture's inadequacies. This conversation turned into a debate with the groundbreaking ministry of Jay Adams. His central contribution to Christian Counseling was a bold and controversial claim that Counseling's task was a theological enterprise that a commitment to God's Word should primarily inform.

Since the 1950s, several different groups have articulated different counseling theories. There have been many different views of how the Christian faith relates to psychology. Each position possesses critical distinctions that create boundaries between the other views. Three groups have emerged: One group is Secular Psychology, which believes that the Bible is entirely irrelevant for Counseling. Another group is Biblical Counseling, which believes that the Bible is sufficient for Counseling. The third group is Christian Counseling (Lambert, pp.3-5). With all these great intentions, where does Christian Counseling miss the mark?

The answer is two-part:

1. Christian Counseling believes it is necessary to augment the Scriptures with secular counseling practices. The position of Christian Counselors (also known as Integrationists) on this matter is exact. Just one example is the work of Mark McMinn. In his book, **Integrative Psychotherapy: Toward a Comprehensive Christian Approach,** which states:

"By way of analogy, consider the temperature system in an automobile. On one end of the continuum is hot air and on the other end is cool air. Often a person selects a temperature in the middle, mixing the hot and cool air for the desired effect. The climate is more desirable and adaptable by combining both air sources than it could be if only one source of air were available.

In this analogy, we are considering two sources of information: Psychology and Christian Faith. To what extent do we let the "air" from both systems mix to achieve an optimal balance? Or should we trust only one source of information and not the other? Reciprocal interaction involves the assumption that caring for people's souls is best done by bringing together the truth from both sources" (McMinn, 23).

McMinn is one of the leading Christian counselors today. He bases his integrative approach on the assumption that it is necessary to add secular counseling techniques to biblical ones to help struggling people. This premise suggests that The Word of God is not sufficient on its own and requires secular techniques to be effective.

> 2. Christian counselors believe that secular counseling strategies are a necessary adjunct to the Bible. They do not believe that the Scriptures are a sufficient counseling resource.

> Stan Jones, a prominent Christian Integrationist, wrote, *"There are many topics to which Scripture does not speak—how neurons work, how the brain synthesizes mathematical or emotional information, the types of memory, or the best way to conceptualize personality traits. Because Scripture and the accumulated wisdom of the Church in theology leave many areas of uncertainty in understanding and helping humanity, we approach psychology expecting that we can learn and grow through our engagement with it."*

> Jones's logic is apparent. Because the Bible lacks information Christian counselors believe to be pertinent to Counseling, they move toward psychology, expecting it to fill in the gaps

("Biblical Counseling vs. Christian Counseling: What's the Difference?" 2020).

Christian Counseling takes the therapies and techniques from Secular Counseling and believes that the Bible is relevant to Counseling but insufficient. What happens when Christian counselors begin with the nomenclature used by secular psychologists? They feel frustrated when they come to Scripture.

The Bible does not address problems they learned in their interaction with the secular psychologies. They are unable to see the Bible's relevance and Christian Counseling is an attempt to serve two masters; in doing so, it fails to heed the warning of Christ in Matthew.

Matt. 6.24,

"No man can serve two masters: for either he will hate the one and love the other; or else he will hold to the one, and despise the other. Ye cannot serve God and mammon."

Christian Counseling is neither hot nor cold; it is lukewarm.

Reset Your Mind!

Romans 12.1-2

"I beseech you therefore, brethren, by the mercies of God, that ye present your bodies a living sacrifice, holy, acceptable unto God, which is your reasonable service.

And be not conformed to this world: but be ye transformed by the renewing of your mind, that ye may prove what is that good, and acceptable, and perfect, will of God."

Introduction

Dr. Duane Gish -
"...the human brain is the most complex arrangement of matter in the universe."

We have an incredible machine inside our head called 'brain.' You may have a high IQ, or average, or even below average intelligence; but your brain is still incredible. Did you know that inside the skull of your head is more information stored than in the national library? That is really incredible for a very small machine that only weighs for about three pounds.

Psychologists tell us that each person has about ten thousand thoughts per day. Did you realize that many thoughts go on inside your head each day? Unbelievable! It means that we have many chances of having good thoughts every day.

This human thought process remains a mystery to scientists and psychologists. But one thing is sure about the mind. How you think will affect the directions of your life and your walk with God.

> *Prov 23.7a,*
> *"For as he thinketh in his heart, so is he:"*

The letter to the believers at Rome, who were predominantly Gentiles, was written around AD57 when Paul was on his third missionary journey. The purpose of the letter was to prepare the way for his coming to Rome, to present the basic gospel of salvation to a church which had not received the teaching of an Apostle before and to explain the relationship between Jew and Gentile in God's overall plan of redemption.

The first 11 chapters of Romans outline the doctrinal teaching of the gospel and as you see in Chapter 12, the first verse begins with the word 'therefore,' linking the practical outworking (which is about to follow) with the doctrine outlined previously. So let us look at Romans Chapter 12.1-2.

Verse 1-

In the first verse – Paul begins this section of his letter with a call for a wholehearted and a whole life commitment to God, in light of His mercy to the believer. We read that Paul 'urges' or beseeches them to offer their *'bodies as sacrifices.'* Note that the NIV has it as *'living sacrifices'* but the Greek literally reads *'offer your bodies as sacrifices, living, holy and pleasing to God.'*

It is significant what Paul asks them to do here. The idea of offering yourself as a sacrifice would have been familiar to the believers in Rome. However, the difference is that instead of an animal being offered to God, it was to be their bodies. Further this was a conscious choice by them; the animal in a sacrifice had no choice. The animal was killed but they were to offer themselves not as those who had died but as living, holy and pleasing to God. This sacrifice of themselves was not a dead one but one full of the energy of life and like all sacrifices they belonged to God and could not be taken back by the giver.

In essence, Paul is saying to them in light of the mercy God has shown you in sending Christ Jesus to die for you, to save you from the wrath of God and eternal damnation, in light of this mercy, you are to offer all that you are, all that you have, every part of your life to God. You no longer belong to yourself but to God!

The recipients of this letter knew that sacrifices were offered morning and evening in the Temple and so they would have understood that Paul was calling them to a daily offering and commitment of their lives to God. This was no once a week offering. This was more than a daily five minutes. The call is to the wholehearted and whole of life commitment to God as a response to His mercy shown in salvation.

Paul concludes verse 1 by saying *"this is your spiritual act of worship."* The daily sacrificing of their lives to God was their 'spiritual act of worship.' This was to be an intelligent and deliberate choice every day for them. The animal sacrifice had no choice, but the people did, and they were to choose every day to surrender their lives to God.

Please note that for Paul 'spiritual worship' had to do with daily living and their daily walk before God – it was not limited to what they did when they came together as the body of believers on Sunday morning.

Verse 2 –

But how were the believers in Rome, and us today, to live such lives of sacrifice? Romans Chapter 12.*2* is one of the most significant verses in all of Paul's letters. Read **verse 2**. The dedicated life is also to be the transformed life. Paul wants them to be able to maintain their commitment to Christ. So often people start out with great commitment to Christ but over time it wanes and some even fall away. Some have lost that initial passion they had for Christ. The flame of faith is almost extinguished. Why? What caused the smothering of our faith? The answer lies in **verse 2**.

What happened was 'conformity' to this world and not 'transformation' in the light of the world to come. Let me explain that to you. Before you came to Christ you lived according to the old man, self, the old Adam. This old Adam was by nature sin and lived according to the flesh by choice. When you came to Christ that was changed by the new birth you no longer live according to the old nature but according to the Spirit of God which is now in you. You are now a co-heir with Christ, a sinner saved by grace with the hope and promise of eternal life in heaven.

But here is where the rubber hits the road – you now must choose to live either according to the Spirit or the flesh. You must choose daily which will be the determining factor in how you live your life each day. Paul says to the believers the challenge is not to conform to the patterns, the sinful ways, or the sinful thinking of this world but to be transformed by the renewing of your minds. How is this done? Well, let me say to you, Paul only uses the word 'transform' on one other occasion in his letters which is in 2 Corinthians 3:18, read – where it speaks of being changed into Christ likeness.

You know the word 'transform' which Paul chooses to use is the same word used to speak of the transfiguration of Christ before the disciples on the mountain. Paul says to the believers at Rome, and to us, that there is to be a conscious renewing of our minds which will transform our lives so that they become sacrifices which are living, holy and pleasing to God. Look at the text closely and you see the way this renewal will transform us – with our minds we understand the patterns of this world which lead us not to transformation, not to daily sacrifice for Christ, but to conformity with this world.

In Galatians 1:4 Paul says that as believers we have been delivered from this present age, whose god is Satan, (2 Cor.4:4) and that we live by the power of the age to come (Heb.6:5), therefore why would we conform to the thinking and the ways of this world. You see Paul understood that in the spiritual life of every believer the battle for control of the mind would ultimately lead to either victory or defeat in daily living. That is why he has spent the first 11 chapters of Romans in his letter outlining doctrine – because what you believe ultimately decides how you live.

The man who believes that success is decided by wealth and possessions will live accordingly. The world cheapens relationships, marriage, family life and people live accordingly. What you think dictates how you live. Psychologists tell us there are two simple rules to do with the mind: The Law of Concentration and the Law of Substitution.

1. In the Law of Concentration, they tell us that whatever we dwell on grows in our life experience and becomes part of us.
2. In the Law of Substitution, they tell us that our conscious mind can only hold one thought at a time, and you can substitute a positive thought for a negative thought and vice versa.

Think about those two laws for a moment in relation to what Paul has just said in Romans 12.2. Can you see how they work out in our thinking and daily life? What you feed your mind with will ultimately be seen in how you live. If you neglect the spiritual food of the mind, then you will end up living a Christian life which is one of weakness and ultimately defeat. Paul says that the conscious renewing of the mind, an ongoing present process, leads to transformation into Christ likeness. We no longer think like an unbeliever. We no longer feed our minds on the things we once did but on things which build us up, strengthen our faith and encourage others. Paul says when we do this, we will be able to discern the will of God for our lives.

So many of us are unsure, ignorant and blind to the will of God – not because you do not want to know it but because you do not have the spiritual mind to know it because you have starved your minds of spiritual food for years. Fashion, the media, popular psychology, folk religion and superstition has changed our lives more than the truth of the gospel.

Practical Application

Let me give you some very practical advice about renewing your mind and transforming your life. I once had a t-shirt which read 'No pain – No gain.' There are no shortcuts to spiritual growth or maturity. There is no easy route to renewing a mind and transforming a life – in fact it is a painful path, and it is a lifelong path.

Here is my advice gained from Scripture and from my own walk with God.

> **First** – You, each day, must consciously surrender your life to Christ. Consciously commit your life to Him every morning. Even Say it out loud, 'Today, I am going to live for You, Lord Jesus Christ.'

> **Secondly** – Daily Prayer and Bible reading is essential if you want to renew your mind, to know the will of God and be transformed. That requires discipline of time, and it requires determination because all sorts of things will demand your time. Make it a priority each day to spend time in God's Word and in God's presence in prayer.

> **Thirdly** – Be in a relationship with at least one other person for spiritual growth. Find someone you can trust; someone you can relate to and invite them to hold you to daily bible reading and prayer. Jesus never sent His disciples out on their own; it was always two by two.

> > ** When Thomas went off on his own, he had to wait another week to see the risen Christ, and he was rebuked for his unbelief.

Finally – Feed your mind with the things that are wholesome. That means Discipline:

- Over What You Watch,
- What You Read,
- What You Listen to in your Media, Social, and Economic Environment,
- What You Say is also most critically important!

Let us be honest – many of you as parents are more protective of what your children view than you are of your own minds and hearts – and yet you are then making decisions, eternal decisions, for yourself and your families.

Wake up! If you fill your mind with the things of this world you will conform to this world and fit into it without a whimper. Let me finish with a promise from God's Word –

Isaiah 26.3,
"3 Thou wilt keep him in perfect peace, whose mind is stayed on thee: because he trusteth in thee.",

That is God's promise to you concerning the renewing of your mind and the transformation of your life.

Conclusion

Remember this:

You control your mind! Renew it daily! Tell your mind to get in line! Tell it to think like Jesus!

It was Jesus who left heaven to come and live among us, to laugh and cry with us.

It was Jesus who taught, healed, and delivered us.

It was Jesus who took all our sins upon Himself.

It was Jesus who carried our sins up a hill called Calvary.

It was Jesus who was nailed to that cross and hung between two thieves.

It was Jesus who hung on that cross for 6 hours.

It was Jesus who died and was buried.

It was Jesus who rose after 3 days and 3 nights.

It was Jesus who returned to heaven to prepare for us.

It will be Jesus who is coming back for His Church! Will you be ready?

God bless you!
Amen.

Make up your mind!

I Kings 18.21

"21 And Elijah came unto all the people, and said, How long halt ye between two opinions? if the Lord be God, follow him: but if Baal, then follow him. And the people answered him not a word."

Introduction

How long will you waver? Ever had a hard time deciding or making a decision? My wife and I play that game when it's time to eat. She'll ask me what I want, and I'll ask her what she wants, and we both say, "Whatever you want." Then I'll say something outrageous, and she'll say, "I don't want that!" Well, make up your mind and say what you want. Now she does!

In the above text, we find the people of God at a very important moment in their lives. Elijah has asked them to make up their minds about whom they will serve. Notice that they didn't say a word. How about you...have you made up your mind about whom you will serve? Let's see if we can see ourselves in this message, let's listen for the voice of God as He speaks to us.

As Christian believers, many times we ask this same question when we are tired from the unbelief state, ignorance and confusion of most people around us. We ask them this same question many times! However, from this story, it seems that sometimes we ourselves can decide for how long this may continue.

1Kings 18.16-24

"So Obadiah went to meet Ahab, and told him. And Ahab went to meet Elijah. When Ahab saw Elijah, Ahab said to him, "Is it you, you troubler of Israel?" And he answered, "I have not troubled Israel, but you have, and your father's house, because you have abandoned the commandments of the LORD and followed the Baals. Now therefore send and gather all Israel to me at Mount Carmel, and the 450 prophets of Baal and the 400 prophets of Asherah, who eat at Jezebel's table." So Ahab sent to all the people of Israel and gathered the prophets together at Mount Carmel. And Elijah came near to all the people and said, "How long will you go limping between two different opinions? If the LORD is God, follow him; but if Baal, then follow him." And the people did not answer him a word. Then Elijah said to the people, "I, even I only, am left a prophet of the LORD, but Baal's prophets are 450 men. Let two bulls be given to us, and let them choose one bull for themselves and cut it in pieces and lay it on the wood, but put no fire to it. And I will prepare the other bull and lay it on the wood and put no fire to it. And you call upon the name of your god, and I will call upon the name of the LORD, and the God who answers by fire, he is God." And all the people answered, "It is well spoken."

How long will you waver? How long will you go limping between two different opinions? The answer is: until you yourself rise for the challenge.

How long will this continue?

I. Until You Stand and Challenge

He was clearly not afraid to challenge them. He planned for it. Tolerating sin never helps but challenging it and those who practice it will bring good results.

> ### 1Ki 18.17-18,
> *"17 When Ahab saw Elijah, Ahab said to him, "Is it you, you troubler of Israel?" 18And he answered, "I have not troubled Israel, but you have, and your father's house, because you have abandoned the commandments of the LORD and followed the Baals".*

> ### Dan 3.16-18,
> *"Shadrach, Meshach, and Abednego answered and said to the king, "O Nebuchadnezzar, we have no need to answer you in this matter. If this be so, our God whom we serve is able to deliver us from the burning fiery furnace, and he will deliver us out of your hand, O king. But if not, be it known to you, O king, that we will not serve your gods or worship the golden image that you have set up."*

> ### Dan 6.10
> *"When Daniel knew that the document had been signed, he went to his house where he had windows in his upper chamber open toward Jerusalem. He got down on his knees three times a day and prayed and gave thanks before his God, as he had done previously."*

II. Until You Stand and Divide

Matthew 10.34-35
"Do not think that I have come to bring peace to the earth. I have not come to bring peace, but a sword. For I have come to set a man against his father, and a daughter against her mother, and a daughter-in-law against her mother-in-law."

1Cor 5:.1,
"But now I am writing to you not to associate with anyone who bears the name of brother if he is guilty of sexual immorality or greed, or is an idolater, reviler, drunkard, or swindler--not even to eat with such a one."

1Cor 5.13
God judges those outside. "Purge the evil person from among you."

Until you repair the altar.

1Kings 18.30"Then Elijah said to all the people, "Come near to me." And all the people came near to him. And he repaired the altar of the LORD that had been thrown down."

Worship and prayers were restored.

1Tim 2.1 "First of all, then, I urge that supplications, prayers, intercessions, and thanksgivings be made for all people, ..."

12 stones representing the 12 tribes of Israel, all has joined.

James 4.8-10 "Draw near to God, and he will draw near to you ... Be wretched and mourn and weep. Let your

59

laughter be turned to mourning and your joy to gloom. Humble yourselves before the Lord, and he will exalt you".

III. Until You Stand Receive the Fire

1 Kings 18.38
"Then the fire of the LORD fell and consumed the burnt offering and the wood and the stones and the dust, and licked up the water that was in the trench."

Until you receive the approval, acceptance and the release of His power.

Luke 24.49
"And behold, I am sending the promise of my Father upon you. But stay in the city until you are clothed with power from on high."

Until you purify – No reform but purification.

1 Kings 18.40
"And Elijah said to them, "Seize the prophets of Baal; let not one of them escape." And they seized them. And Elijah brought them down to the brook Kishon and slaughtered them there."

Col 3.5
"Put to death therefore what is earthly in you: sexual immorality, impurity, passion, evil desire, and covetousness, which is idolatry."

For how long you will miss your chance of doing something? For how long you will keep them wavering? For how long you will continue to be silent?

> *Jer 1.6-7*
> *"Then I said, "Ah, Lord GOD! Behold, I do not know how to speak, for I am only a youth." But the LORD said to me, "Do not say, 'I am only a youth'; for to all to whom I send you, you shall go, and whatever I command you, you shall speak."*

Conclusion

Church, make up your mind! Time is running out! The Word of God tells us that one day Jesus is coming back for His church. Will you be in that church? I tell you this: if you have not made up your mind you will not be in that church!

Jesus died on the cross so that we may have eternal life. Have you made that sacrifice null and void? If you haven't made up your mind, what are you waiting for? It's not complicated! Make up your mind whether or not you're going to serve God of Satan! I pray that you choose God. God bless you!

Amen.

Biblical Counseling

Biblical Counseling (also known as nouthetic Counseling) gets its name from the Greek word Noutheteo, which translates as "admonish" (Rom. 15.14). It means "to confront as a friend" and was the standard Counseling method before modernists invented secular psychology in the early 1900s. A study of older dictionaries shows that it took until 1973 for the word "counseling" to change from "giving advice" to "psychology" with its modern testing, processes, and therapies. That change gradually came about as the secular psychology influence changed our idea of Counseling from a pastor to that given by a secular psychologist.

History of Biblical Counseling

During the mid-20th century, many Christians thought they could integrate secular theory into their counseling programs, mixing the Bible with psychology. That practice (called "Christian" Counseling) on the false assumption that man can discover God's truth apart from the Bible. In the late 1960s, several godly pastors saw the need to reject such damaging influences. One man (Dr. Jay Adams) led the way in bringing biblical Counseling back into pastoral ministry. While psychology works on evolution and secular philosophy, Biblical Counseling is based strictly on biblical principles. For Counseling to be biblical, it must be Bible-based, Christ-centered, and local church-oriented. Nouthetic Counseling accepts the premise that the Bible is God's Word (2 Tim. 3.16-17) and that it is sufficient for meeting all our needs (2 Peter 1.3-4) (What is nouthetic Counseling? 2021).

Declare your mind!

Joshua 24.15

"15 And if it seem evil unto you to serve the Lord, choose you this day whom ye will serve; whether the gods which your fathers served that were on the other side of the flood, or the gods of the Amorites, in whose land ye dwell: but as for me and my house, we will serve the Lord."

INTRODUCTION

My friends, what we need today is for families to get together, have family conversations/discussions. People are lonely and downhearted because nobody in the family wants to listen. They are all busy and they are not sensitive to the situations.

That is why our teenagers nowadays are looking for something outside the family that will fill-in the void that is inside of them … what do we see and read in the newspaper, young boys hooked up on drugs … teenage girls getting pregnant … by who?

We cannot change the fact that according to statistics, US now belongs to the top ten in drugs and abortion. And this is a prevalent practice in our society probably because the very nucleus of this society (the family) is neglected and taken for granted. What is your family doing in this kind of situations?

Again why, not only the breadwinners are busy but also the government so much has pampered our children.

Yes, on some occasions you can impose discipline but is limited because the moment your hands hurt them physically, in a couple of minutes or hours or so… there you go, the best cop in town is knocking on your door and inviting you not to a dinner date but interrogation in the police department.

But I tell you even if the society or the government fails to accomplish its duties, God will not. We can lean on Him, and I will assure you that He is also working non-stop to lead us in the path of perfection.

Joshua penned this deathless statement when he said, *"But as for me and my house, we will serve the Lord."*

Joshua was right and he made the greatest decision a father could decide for his family… Joshua will never regret his decision that he and his family will serve the Lord God.

I believe one of the reasons why the society has gone astray or lost because the real and true God - Jesus Christ is out of the picture of our life. He is no longer part of the family portrait. We need to go back to the basic and undo or refresh what was forgotten for a long time … that is, to serve the Lord and teach our children the reward of allowing God to work in our midst.

I am very sure that we all have heard the statement; *"the family that prays together stays together."* I am proud to say this phrase is true to our family because since we learned how to pray- we have a family devotion, and we are praying together every morning before our children get on the school bus. Aside from watching movies and football together … add to it the topics about life - its meaning and purpose and most especially spiritual things. We need to start now; or it may never happen, or it will be too late.

Every day all of us face many decisions that range from trivial to very important ones. When you get up in the morning it is a new day that God, Himself has given to you that could possibly have an outcome that can affect the rest of your life. There are those decisions that we make that will affect us in a positive way and in a negative way.

Today we will refer to two different crossroads that can have the cause-and-effect syndrome in life. The positive road is the road to achieving godly success, and the negative road we will classify as dead-end decisions.

Our text gives us the perfect Biblical example that when we make the wrong decisions it WILL affect us in a negative way.

The first cause and effect of a dead-end decision is:

I. TINY TENDENCIES

A tendency is likelihood to move, thinks, or act in a particular way. As we look behind the history of this text when Joshua told the people to choose, it puts into our mind the tendencies that they had with the leader Moses that was before Joshua. At first their tendencies were not that big of a deal. Right? WRONG! Let's look at a few tiny tendencies that they had that caused some dead-end decisions to be made.

The murmuring (low indistinct sound)

In the book of Exodus, chapters 16-17 gives us a history of the tendencies that the children of Israel had.

- ✓ God provided manna from heaven
- ✓ They enjoyed it for a while and then begin to complain about it
- ✓ God sent them quail from heaven
- ✓ They enjoyed it for a while and then began to complain about it.
- ✓ Then the Bible states that they had a fight with their leader Moses in *Exodus 17:2* about wanting water.
- ✓ After the meal that God had provided, they said to Moses why have you brought us out here in the dessert to die?
- ✓ So, God said to Moses take some of the leaders and strike the rock at Horeb and water will come out to drink.
- ✓ The place was called Massah and Meribah because they tested the Lord by saying is the Lord among us or not?
- ✓ Massah means testing and Meribah means quarreling. Some people just can't be satisfied.

5. These tiny tendencies of murmuring caused them not to cross over to their inheritance.

6. God told Moses that because of these tendencies they could not cross.

7. The children of Israel were at a dead end because of a dead-end decision!

8. What about you? Do you have any tiny tendencies that are causing dead end decisions in your life?

The second cause and effect of a dead-end decision is:

II. TREACHEROUS TRADITIONS

1. What can cause a major dead-end decision in our life?

2. Jesus was not just dealing with murmuring and complains but he was dealing with traditions that were taught by men.

3. Things that are traditional that we deal with in the Church that have caused the Church abroad to make bad decisions:

The day and time of worship in the Church

The type of music in the Church

The type of outward appearance in the Church

The words or phrases we use in the Church

The style of the building itself

The list goes on and on!

4. Jesus was dealing with the same Spirit recorded in Matthew 15, look at verses 10-11

5. Joshua knew that the children of Israel had a tendency to make dead end decisions because of their treacherous traditions.

6. He would have to lead them in a way that he could communicate that God looks at the heart and not the outward!

7. The only way out of bad traditions is to teach what the purpose is.

8. If the tradition still works and has a defined purpose, then it should still be implemented.

9. If it doesn't then it should be trashed, and a new fresh new vision is needed!

The next cause and effect is what we cannot keep from happening, but God CAN heal:

III. TRANSFORMING TRAUMAS

The children of Israel did go through some serious loses throughout the years of things, family, friends, etc. that caused them to make dead end decisions. When it seems that our hope is gone, we make dead end decisions. The fact is, when we are in the worst of traumas, we must eventually come out of them so that we can think clearly to make right choices and decisions.

There are some Biblical examples of people that went through traumas that did and did not make it:

Judas did not make it

Jesus did make it

Mary the mother of Jesus did make it

The rich man did not make it.

Traumas can cause anyone to make dead end decisions, but we must get through them. The man with no feet thanked God he had legs! All of these things (Tiny Tendencies, Treacherous Traditions, and Transforming Traumas) can cause dead end decisions.

Joshua stood up as recorded in *Joshua 24.14-15* and told them to make the right decision and not dead decisions!

The way we make the right decisions in the face of tendencies, traditions and traumas is to accept:

IV. TRIUMPHAL TRUTH

I Corinthians 2.13 States, "This is what we speak, not in words taught us by human wisdom but in words taught by the Spirit, expressing spiritual truths in spiritual words."

The choices that you make such as:

The choice to be free from the Tiny Tendencies that bind you.

The choice to know God's truth instead of the Treacherous Traditions you have been taught.

The choice to get through the Transforming traumas of life.

These choices can only be made through the Triumphal Truth of God's word! Jesus said I AM the way.

Fathers, you are being held responsible for your families, especially their spiritual life. 1 Tim 5.8 says, *"But if any provide not for his own, and especially for those of his own house, he hath denied the faith, and is worse than an infidel."* An infidel is an unbeliever.

We have fathers who take their families to church, drop them off, and the father goes back home.

We have fathers who go to one church and their wife and children go to another church and they think everything's all right, but

Jesus said in Matt 12.25, *"And Jesus knew their thoughts, and said unto them, every kingdom divided against itself is brought to desolation; and every city or house divided against itself shall not stand."*

We have some unstable fathers who will come to church, rededicate their lives to God, and then disappear. They're unstable. We have fathers who say they want the church to grow but only the way they want it to, not anybody else's.

My sisters don't think I've forgotten about you. If you're a single parent, it's up to you to declare that as for you and your house you will serve the Lord.

God is looking for the men of every church in the sound of my voice to stand up and be counted. Stand up in your house stand up in God's house.

Jesus has shown us the way. He paid for our sins with His own blood. He loved the Church as gave His life for it. This is how men should love their wives. My brothers, be the Man God created you to be and lead your family in serving God. Be the Man God created you to be to lead your family to Christ! Declare in your mind whom you're going to serve! Amen.

Comparison of Counseling Methods

Biblical Counseling vs. Secular Counseling

All psychologies have an epistemology: they have some theory of knowledge, and with Secular Counseling, this is true. The question is not regarding the existence of epistemology but the existence of biblical epistemology. The significance because one cannot make authoritative claims of right and wrong, claims about changing human motivation and the purpose of life, or what behavior should look like without having some implicit commitment to knowledge and truth. Biblical Counseling sees the Scripture as the final authority of truth and how we know the truth (John 17.17).

The approaches used in secular Counseling are in disarray. There are many schools of psychology, and some methods are in total disagreement with each other. Worse, there is no central focus on absolute truth in the secular psychological approach. Man develops and defines his idea of "truth," so there are few absolutes; values are relative, frequently changing, and fluctuating. The labeling and confronting of sin are actions that would diminish self-esteem. There is no realization that emotional problems are spiritual problems caused by personal sin.

Secular psychology is based on man's ideas and uses a relative system based on the World's client's and the psychologist's values. It has no recognition of or needs to adhere to God's whole value system or morals. The counselor often encourages the client to seek his solutions and is often "non-directive."

Biblical Counseling operates on God's ideas and a whole value system, the Scriptures, which never vary as society's views change. Biblical Counseling is highly directive because God Himself is directive. It is also confrontational as Christ and his apostles were confrontational (Secular vs. Biblical Counseling Part One, 2021).

Biblical Counseling establishes the premise that emotional problems are usually spiritual problems and that submission to Christ and His Word is the solution to man's problems caused by his sin. It stands on the directions, promises, and concepts of God, imparted through His Word, the Scriptures. The Bible is a guidebook on how to develop a proper relationship with God and others. God designs the Scriptures to bring change in the believer (Peter 1:3,4, John 17:17). The purposes of Scripture are in Timothy 3:16-17: teaching, rebuking, correcting, training in righteousness, and equipping the believer.

Biblical Counseling vs. Christian Counseling

Many will say that their Counseling is Christian and biblical, but the test evaluates what they do when counseling. The issue is whether one incorporates other beliefs and practices or not. Nouthetic Counseling is based entirely upon Scripture. Other systems, claiming to be, are not. When one gets right down to examining what people do in Counseling, it is quite evident that their claims are false. That is how it differs from other counseling systems that claim to be Christian. It warrants the claim to the name "Christian" and the name "Biblical." In doing this, the Bible becomes an illustration book from which people take materials to "back" their beliefs. Because they use much Bible-wrongly interpreted and used for purposes for which it was never intended-what they have to say may impress the unwary as being quite Christian. However, the fact is there is nothing fundamentally Christian or biblical about the temperament theory at all. Indeed, to call it such is a deception of the rawest sort. Christians need to become far more discerning and not accept whatever claims to be Christian as such. Unless the system is biblical from start to finish, it is not Christian (How does Nouthetic Counseling differ from other forms of Christian Counseling? 2021).

Nouthetic Counseling is a refreshing return to a strictly biblical method of problem-solving. Instead of focusing on the problem and expecting years of therapy, nouthetic Counseling focuses on the biblical solution. It expects the counselee to change by the Holy Spirit's power—conforming to the biblical model presented (Romans 828-29). Nouthetic Counseling is effective for believers and begins with the evangelism of those who are not believers because biblical counselors understand that only believers can understand God's profound truths (1 Corinthians 2.14). Since all believers have the Holy Spirit and God's Word to change them (1 Corinthians 6.9-11; Galatians 5.16), Biblical (nouthetic) Counseling depends on the Holy Spirit to change the believer, using God's Word as it is—to teach, rebuke, correct and train in righteousness (2 Timothy 3.16).

The future of Biblical Counseling

There are few colleges and seminaries that teach nouthetic Counseling today. However, the list is growing, as more and more Christians are seeing the weakness and error in trying to integrate secular thought with the Bible. Colossians 2.8 says, *"Beware lest anyone cheat you through philosophy and empty deceit, according to the tradition of men, according to the basic principles of the world, and not according to Christ"* (NKJV). That is the dividing line between Biblical (nouthetic) Counseling, Christian Counseling, and Secular Psychology.

Today Biblical Counseling is a significant force among conservative American Protestants. It is so popular and so widespread that in 2005 the Southern Baptist Convention's theological seminaries—the religious schools of the largest Protestant denomination in the country—announced a "wholesale change of emphasis" in favor of Biblical Counseling. This change was over an earlier "pastoral care" model drawn in part on the behavioral sciences.

Accreditation organizations like the Association of Certified Biblical Counselors have certified just over 1,000 counselors to date—but Biblical Counseling does not require accreditation. Indirectly, the influence of Biblical Counseling is broader still and echoes across conservative culture. In 2012, Adam Lanza slaughtered a school full of children in Connecticut. Fox News host and onetime GOP presidential hopeful Mike Huckabee, a former Southern Baptist pastor himself, slipped into Biblical Counseling territory. He blamed the killings in part on a society in which we "stop saying things are sinful and we call them disorders." Furthermore, Southern Baptist research organization Lifeway Research surveyed evangelical Christians in 2013. Forty-eight percent of self-identified evangelical, born-again, or fundamentalist Christians said they believe that conditions like bipolar disorder and schizophrenia can be treated by prayer alone (The Rise of Biblical Counseling, 2012).

Nevertheless, Biblical Counseling also faces serious difficulties. It confronts mounting external criticisms and widening internal divisions, and the result, among its practitioners, is a looming crisis of principle. How Christians address this crisis will shape the mental health choices of millions of Americans.

CHAPTER FIVE

METHODOLOGY

A 10-question survey was administered to several local Counselors, Christian Counselors, and Local Pastors (see Appendix A). The survey contained questions that attempted to reveal the following:

1. Their chosen method of Counseling.

2. How long they have been counseling.

3. What are their counseling credentials.

4. Do they feel their credentials are adequate for what they do.

5. The foundation of their Counseling is based.

6. Their opinions of the other two counseling methods.

7. Are they open to the other two counseling methods?

8. The counselor's definition of "sin" and "sickness."

9. The counselor's definition of alcoholism, sexual addiction, and bipolar disorder.

10. Does the Counselor classify alcoholism, sexual addiction, and bipolar disorder as sickness or sin.

In my local area there are over sixty local Churches and two Counseling Centers with five Secular/Christian counselors in each one. In this study, fifteen Pastors and five Counselors were randomly mailed a survey and had two weeks to complete and return it.

Using the computer program Survey Monkey for this statistical analysis, it provided the answers used to analyze, interpret, and debate the various psychological and clinical words and phrases used to redefine sin. The project depicted multiple variables and sought to determine a relationship between these variables using numbers, surveys, and charts. Therefore, the quantitative method was used in the furtherance of this book. If there were no responses, statistical data from peer articles and journals would serve as plan "B." A total of 20 surveys were mailed out. This number represented 25% of the Biblical and 25% of the Secular and Christian Counselors. Of the 20 surveys mailed out, 18 were received. Two of the surveys mailed to churches were returned stamped "No Forwarding Address."

CHAPTER SIX

RESULTS

The first five questions of the survey provide background information about the counselor. Three identified as Secular Counselors (one as a Psychologist at the Doctorate level, two at the master's level), four identified as Christian Counselors, and eleven identified as Pastors.

Questions 6 and 7 to determine how the counselor views and considers the other two counseling methods. Questions 8-10 were the heart of the survey. These questions reflected the counselor's definition of sin, their source for defining three sins/sicknesses (Alcoholism, Kleptomania, and Bipolar Disorder), and the impact of such definitions on the Church. The survey answered all the sought-after questions (see Appendix B). The following answers are from focused questions according to the counseling method.

Secular Counselors

Question 8

How do you define sin and sickness?

Were split 50-50 when defining sin and sickness with answers being either B. "Sin is evil acts, whether of thought or of deed; Sickness is an unhealthy condition of body and mind or state of being ill" or C. "Sin is a transgression against Devine law; Sickness is an unhealthy condition of body and mind. "

Question 9

What would you use to define 'Alcoholism,' 'Kleptomania,' and 'Bipolar Disorder'?

100% use the DSM-5 to define as sickness what the Bible defines as sin.

Question 10

When the Church starts calling 'Sin' 'Sickness,' it no longer needs a Savior; it needs a therapist?

100% agree that the Church needs a therapist when it redefines sin as sickness.

Christian Counselors

Question 8

How do you define sin and sickness?

75% believe sin to be a transgression against Devine law or evil acts, and that sickness is an unhealthy condition of body and mind or state of being ill.

Question 9

What would you use to define 'Alcoholism,' 'Kleptomania,' and 'Bipolar Disorder'?

They were split equally (33%) among those who answered the question concerning what resource to use in classifying the three sins/sicknesses that are listed.

Question 10

When the Church starts calling 'Sin' ' Sickness,' it no longer needs a Savior; it needs a therapist. Agree or Disagree

Were split equally (25%) concerning if the Church needs a therapist or a savior.

Biblical Counselors

Question 8

How do you define sin and sickness?

**40% defined sin and sickness as C.

> "Sin is a transgression against Devine law; Sickness is an unhealthy condition of body and mind."

**30% said sin and sickness as A.

> "Sin is a transgression against Devine law; Sickness is the state of being ill."

**20% defined them as D.

> "Sin is evil acts, whether of thought or of deed; Sickness is the state of being ill."

**10% defined them as B.

> "Sin is evil acts, whether of thought or of deed; Sickness is the state of being ill; Sickness is an unhealthy condition of body and mind."

Question 9

What would you use to define 'Alcoholism,' 'Kleptomania,' and 'Bipolar Disorder'?

**20% would use the DSM-5

**10% would use a combination of the Holy Bible and the DSM-5.

Question 10

When the Church starts calling "Sin" Sickness," it no longer needs a Savior; it needs a therapist?

**50% Strongly Agree

**20% Agree with the statement

**20% Strongly Disagree

**10% Disagree

CHAPTER SEVEN

DISCUSSION

The survey reveals the following:

1. The counseling methods currently available to the Church.

2. The counseling method's philosophy

3. The counseling method's view of the other methods

4. How each counseling method defines sin and sickness.

5. The view from each counseling method concerning the Church's need for a savior or a therapist.

There are currently three counseling methods available to the Church: Secular Counseling (Man can heal himself with help from the DSM), Christian Counseling (man can use the Bible, but needs the DSM to cover where the Bible is silent), and Biblical Counseling that believes that the Holy Bible is sufficient to heal man of his problems.

The survey revealed that only one counselor (Christian Counselor) has been counseling for less than five years. The majority have been counselors who have been counseling for over 15 years, with Biblical Counselors at 60%. All counselors agreed that the training they have received was adequate for the method of Counseling they practice.

Question 5 dealt with the subject of the counseling foundation. The numbers for Secular Counseling and Christian Counseling fell where expected: Modern Psychology for Secular Counseling and Modern Psychology and the Holy Bible for Christian Counselors. The surprise was with Biblical Counselors. 60% said their Counseling stands on the Holy Bible, but 40% said they would use both the Holy Bible and Modern Psychology. This number (40%) should raise red flags and sound all the alarms. The Church is leaning in the direction of Christian Counseling.

The past twenty-years have seen many Christian Counseling advances (*Putting Christ Back into Christian Counseling, 2021*). The Church believes that the Holy Bible is not totally sufficient to heal man. This shifting mindset is weakening the Church.

About their view of the other counseling methods, both Secular and Christian Counselors gave the expected answers. Again, Biblical Counselors are divided on the effectiveness of the other two methods. 80% believe that both Secular and Christian Counseling is either Extremely Effective (10%), Very Effective (20%), or somewhat effective (50%). Only 20% stated that the other two counseling methods were Not so Effective. The bright spot of hope was how Biblical Counselors were nearly united as 60% stated that they were unlikely or doubtful to consider using Secular or Christian Counseling. Once again, this should be alarming. The percentage should have been higher. The Church has drifted away from the authority and the effectiveness of the Holy Bible.

The answers to **Question 8**, *"How do you define sin and sickness?"* were predictable for both Secular and Christian Counselors. As observed earlier with **Question 5**, the Biblical Counselors were varied. 70% defined sin as "a transgression," and 30% defined it as "evil acts." Biblical Counselors were evenly split (50-50) on the definition of sickness. Both Secular and Christian Counselors were united in their definitions.

Again, Secular Counselors were united in answering their reference source for defining the given sin/sicknesses. Christian Counselors evenly responded to the first three answer choices. Biblical Counselors were vital here, with 70% referring to the Holy Bible to define the sins/sicknesses used in the survey. However, 20% would refer to the DSM, and 10% stated they would use both the Holy Bible and the DSM.

For the last question, all counselor methods were either in agreement or disagreement concerning the Church's condition once calling sin sickness. Secular Counselors agreed with the statement. Christian Counselors were 50-50 (agree or disagree). Biblical Counselors were 70% in agreement with the statement, and 30% disagreed.

What do these results say? **The Church is in trouble!** While Secular and Christian Counseling were more in agreement in their responses, Biblical Counselors were varied. Their varying answers show a lack of unity. Biblical Counselors are beginning to merge with Christian Counselors f this trend continues, Biblical Counseling will become a thing of the past. The Bible will no longer be considered sufficient; it will have to stand next to the DSM for credibility. The implications are readily apparent. Before the Covid-19 pandemic, churches were open for service. Once Covid-19 became a pandemic, churches were closed, and nearly all are still closed with services held via the internet. If ever there was a time for the Church to let its light shine, it is now! People are looking for answers. The Church has the answers; the answers are in the Word of God, the Holy Bible.

These results are not absolute. The number of participants was limited to the availability of the chosen methods of Counseling. In a larger metropolitan city, the sample size would have been larger. However, this does not diminish the results that are provided. This survey is a snapshot of what is happening in and to the Church at this very moment. It is up to the Church to rediscover itself. As Jesus said to the Church at Ephesus,

"4 Nevertheless I have somewhat against thee, because thou hast left thy first love. 5 Remember therefore from whence thou art fallen, and repent, and do the first works; or else I will come unto thee quickly, and will remove thy candlestick out of his place, except thou repent"

(Rev. 2.4-5). The Church needs to return to her first love, Christ, and call sin!

CHAPTER EIGHT

SUMMARY

This work alerts the Church that there is cancer within it. This cancer does not have a medical name. Considering the deadly effects, it has and will continue to have on its members, the Church should call this cancer "SOS" ("Sin or Sickness"). Although SOS officially is just a distinctive Morse code sequence that is not an abbreviation for anything, in widespread usage, it is associating with phrases such as "Save Our Souls" and "Save Our Ship." Moreover, due to its high-profile use in emergencies, the phrase "SOS" has entered general usage to indicate a crisis or the need for action informally.

There are three counseling options that church members can choose from Secular, Christian, and Biblical. The Church has the moral responsibility to inform its members of the dangers of choosing Secular and even Christian Counseling in helping them with life's problems. For Christians, Biblical Counseling is the answer.

CHAPTER NINE

CONCLUSION

This research exposes the danger of the Church calling sin sickness. The research answered some key questions. These answers include the following: The Church began adopting psychological concepts in the 1960s with Christian Counseling. This hybrid counseling method combines both Secular and Christian principles. This adoption has led the Church to hire counselors to their staff who may not view the Holy Bible as being sufficient to heal the Church's congregation's problems. The research found that the Church has become politically correct by using Humanistic Psychology's vocabulary by classifying sin as sickness.

The Church must make some serious decisions: whose doctrine and which Worldview will it embrace? These decisions have the Church in a place it should never be. This place is one of confusion. The confusion comes from the Church moving away from the Holy Bible's authority and adopting the Secular Worldview. Under the disguise of Christian Counseling, the Church has allowed the Secular Worldview to infiltrate and plant the seeds of doubt and confusion into its congregations' hearts and minds. If not quickly plucked out, these seeds take root and will grow into trees of despair.

The survey is but a small sample of three chosen sins as defined in the Holy Bible. More research on a larger scale is recommended to quantify these answers. Counseling is necessarily theological, based on the Word of God. Engaging in counseling practice is a theological engagement. Evaluating and debating with various counseling practitioners, whether secular, Christian, or biblical, is a theological enterprise.

Works Cited

"Alcoholism," Wikipedia, 27 May 2020, www.wikipedia.org/wiki/Alcoholism. Accessed

27 May 2020.

American Psychiatric Association Diagnostic and Statistical Manual of Mental

Disorders, DSM- 5. Arlington, Virginia: American Psychiatric Publishing; 2013.

"Bipolar Disorder," Web MD, www.webmd.com/bipolar-disorder/mental-health-bipolar-

disorder#1. Accessed 17 June 2020.

Caplan, Paula J, They Say You're Crazy: How the World's Most Powerful Psychiatrists

Decide Who's Normal, Perseus Books, Reading, MA, 1995, p. xv.

Ibid, xvi.

Chavez, Hector Oswald, "Christian Counseling versus Secular Counseling," News,

www.alabamagazette.com/story/2016/05/01/news/christian-counseling-versus-secular-counseling/750.html. Accessed 27 May 2020.

"Christian Counseling vs. Secular Counseling," CCU online,

https://www.ccu.edu/blogs/cags/2010/11/christian-counseling-vs-secular-counseling/#:~:text=Christian%20counseling%20is%20distinct%20from,will%20in%20an%20individual's%20life.&text=By%20using%20biblical%20concepts%20in,provide%20specific%20direction%20and%20accountability. Accessed 30 December 2020.

"Christian Counseling," Wikipedia,

https://en.wikipedia.org/wiki/Christian_counseling#:~:text=The%20aim%20of%2

0Christian%20counseling,the%20Holy%20Spirit's%20convictio n. Accessed 30

December 2020.

 "C.S. Lewis and Sigmund Freud A Comparison of Their Thoughts and Viewpoints on

Life, Pain and Death," Independent Institute,

https://www.independent.org/publications/article.asp?id=1668. Accessed 27

October 2020.

"Darwin and Freud," https://www.sparknotes.com/lit/sophie/section13/. Accessed 27

October 2020.

"Diagnostic and Statistical Manual of Mental Disorders." Wikipedia, The Free

Encyclopedia,

https://en.wikipedia.org/wiki/Diagnostic_and_Statistical_Manua l_of_Mental_Dis-

orders 8. Accessed 17 December 2020.

Frey, Dennis D, Biblical Directionism, GMA & Inspiration Press, Newburgh, IN, 2003,

p. iii.

"History of Counseling Psychology," Psychology,

http://psychology.iresearchnet.com/counseling-psychology/history-of-counseling-

psychology/. Accessed 29 December 2020.

"How does Nouthetic Counseling differ from other forms of Christian Counseling?",

Institute for Nouthetic Studies, http://www.nouthetic.org/how-does-nouthetic- counseling-differ-from-other-forms-of-christian-counseling. Accessed 09 January,

2021.

"Is Psychology Needed in the Church?" Learn Theology, https://learnthelogy.com/is-

psychology-needed-in-the-church.html. Accessed 07 September 2020.

Kräupl, Taylor F, The Concepts of Disease, Illness and Morbus, Cambridge: Cambridge

University Press, 1979, p. 11.

Lambert, Heath, and Stuart Scott, Counseling the Hard Cases, B&H Publishing,

Nashville, TN, pp. 3-5.

Langham, R.Y, "Christian Counseling," Therapy Tribe,

www.therapytribe.com/therapy/christian-counseling. Accessed 21 May 2020.

"Literally," Dictionary.com,
https://www.dictionary.com/browse/literally?s=t. Accessed

27 October 2020.

Mack, Wayne A, "What is Biblical Counseling?" Totally
Sufficient, Ed Hindson &

Howard Eyrich, Harvest House Publishers, Eugene, OR, 1997,
p. 25.

"Psychology and the Church (Part One)," Christian Resource
Institute,

https://www.equip.org/article/psychology-and-the-church-part-
one/. Accessed 07 September 2020.

"Putting Christ back into Christian Counseling," Sagemont
Church, https://www.sagemontchurch.org/article/putting-christ-
back-into-christian-counseling/.

Accessed 16 February 2021.

"Secular," Merriam-Webster, https://www.merriam-
webster.com/dictionary/secular.

Accessed 29 December 2020.

"Secular vs Biblical Counseling Part One," Runny Meade
School,

https://runnymedeschool.com/secular-vs-biblical-counseling-
part-one/. Accessed

09 January 2021.

"Stress," Merriam-Webster, https://www.merriam-
webster.com/dictionary/stress.

Accessed 17 December 2020.

"The Beginnings of Mental Illness," American Psychological Association,

https://www.apa.org/monitor/2012/02/mental-illness#. Accessed 17 December

2020.

Thompson-Chain Reference Bible, King James Version, Kirkbride Bible Company,

Indianapolis, IN, 2007.

Tyler, David, and Kurt Grady, Deceptive Diagnosis, Bemidji, MN, 2006, p. 53.

Tyler, David M, God's Funeral, Focus Publishing, Bemidji, MN, 2009, p.2.

"What Are The Differences Between Christian Counseling And Secular Counseling?", My Therapist, https://www.mytherapist.com/advice/counseling/what-are-the-differences-

between-christian-counseling-and-secular-counseling/. Accessed 29 December

2020.

"What is Christian Counseling Versus Secular Counseling," Mimosa Christian

Counseling Center, https://mimosachristiancounseling.org/faqs/christian-counseling-versus-secular-counseling/. Accessed 29 December 2020.

"What is nouthetic counseling?", Got Questions, https://www.gotquestions.org/nouthetic-

counseling.html. Accessed 09 January 2021.

Wood, Garth, The Myth of Neurosis, Harper & Row, New York, NY, 1983, p.70.

Zuckerman, Phil, "What Does "Secular" Mean?", Psychology Today,

https://www.psychologytoday.com/us/blog/the-secular-life/201407/what-does-

secular-mean. Accessed 29 December 2020.

Bibliography

Adams, Jay E. A Theology of Christian Counseling, Grand Rapids: Zondervan, 1986. Print.

Adams, Jay E. Helps for Counselors: A Mini-Manual for Christian Counseling, Grand Rapids: Baker Book House, 1980. Print.

Adams, Jay E. How to Help People Change: The Four-Step Biblical Process, Grand Rapids: Zondervan, 1986. Print.

Adams, Jay E. Ready to Restore the Layman's Guide to Christian Counseling, Phillipsburg: P & R, 1992. Print.

Adams, Jay E. The Christian Counselor's Manual, Grand Rapids: Zondervan, 1986. Print.

Anderson, Neil. Discipleship Counseling, Bloomington: Baker Group, 2003. Print.

Clinton, Tim, and Ron Hawkins. Quick-Reference Guide to Biblical Counseling, Ada: Baker, 2009. Web. 2020.

Clinton, Timothy E., and Ronald E. Hawkins. The Popular Encyclopedia of Christian

Counseling: An Indispensable Tool for Helping People with Their Problems, Eugene: Harvest House, 2011. Print.

Clinton, Timothy E., and Ronald E. Hawkins. The Quick-reference Guide to Biblical

Counseling: Personal and Emotional Issues, Grand Rapids: Baker, 2009. Print.

Cobb, Larry. Effective Biblical Counseling: A Model for Helping Caring Christians Become Capable Counselors, Grand Rapids: Zondervan, 2014. Web. 2020.

Collins, Gary R. Christian Counseling, Revised and Updated. Third ed, Nashville: Thomas Nelson, 2006. Print.

Fraser, J. Cameron. Developments in Biblical Counseling, Grand Rapids: Reformation Heritage, 2015. Print.

Frey, Dennis. Biblical Directionism, Newburgh: GMA & Inspiration, 2003. Print.

Gingrich, Heather David, and Fred C. Gingrich. Treating Trauma in Christian Counseling, Downers Grove: IVP Academic, an Imprint of InterVarsity, 2017. Print.

Hindson, Ed, and Howard Eyrich. Totally Sufficient, Eugene: Harvest House, 1997. Print.

Hunt, June. The Biblical Counseling Reference Guide, Eugene: Harvest House, 2014. Print.

Jones, Ian F. The Counsel of Heaven on Earth: Foundations for Biblical Christian Counseling, Nashville: B&H Academic, 2018. Print.

Kellemen, Bob. Biblical Counseling and the Church: God's Care Through God's People, Grand Rapids: Zondervan, 2015. Print.

Lambert, Heath. A Theology of Biblical Counseling: The Doctrinal Foundations of Counseling Ministry, Grand Rapids: Zondervan, 2016. Print.

Lambert, Heath. Course Guide for A Theology of Biblical Counseling, Grand Rapids:

Zondervan, 2020. Print.

Lambert, Heath, The Biblical Counseling Movement after Adams (Forward by David Powlison), Wheaton: Crossway, 2011. Print.

Lane, Timothy S, and Paul David Tripp. How People Change, Greensboro: New Growth, 2008. Print.

Lelek, Jeremy. Biblical Counseling: Basics, Roots, Beliefs, and Future, Greensboro: New

Growth, 2018. Print.

Malony, H. Newton, and David W. Augsburger. Christian Counseling: An Introduction,

Nashville: Abingdon, 2007. Print.

Marrs, Rick W. Making Christian Counseling More Christ-Centered, Bloomington: Westbow, 2019. Print.

McMinn, Mark R. Psychology, Theology, and Spirituality in Christian Counseling, Carol

Stream: Tynsdale House, 2011. Print.

McMinn, Mark R. Sin and Grace in Christian Counseling, Downers Grove: InterVarsity, 2008. Print.

Mohler, R. Albert. God and the Gay Christian? A Response to Matthew Vines, Louisville: SBTS, 2014. Print.

Nicholls, Andrew, Helen Thorne, and David Powlison. Real Change: Becoming More

Like Jesus in Everyday Life, Greensboro: New Growth, 2018. Print.

Powlison, David. Seeing with New Eyes, Phillipsburg: P&R, 2003. Print.

Ross, George R. Evaluating Models of Christian Counseling, Eugene: Wipf & Stock, 2011. Print.

Sanders, Randolph K. Christian Counseling Ethics: A Handbook for Psychologists, Therapists and Pastors, Downers Grove: InterVarsity Academic, 2013. Print.

Scott, Stuart, and Heath Lambert. Counseling the Hard Cases: True Stories Illustrating the Sufficiency of God's Resources in Scripture, Nashville: B&H, 2012. Print.

Shaw, Mark E. Strength in Numbers: The Team Approach to Biblical Counseling, Bemidji: Focus, 2010. Print.

Smith, Chuck. Biblical Counseling: A Topical Index for Christian Living, Alpharetta: Word for Today, 2016. Print.

Stanford, Matthew S. Grace for the Afflicted: A Clinical and Biblical Perspective on Mental Illness, Downers Grove, IL: IVP, an Imprint of InterVarsity, 2017. Print.

Stevens, Becca. The Gift of Compassion: Helping Those That Grieve, Nashville: Abingdon, 2012. Print.

Tracy, Steven R., Celestia G. Tracy, and Kristi Ickes Garrison. Mending the Soul:

Understanding and Healing Abuse, Grand Rapids, MI: Zondervan, 2008. Print.

Tyler, David, and Kurt Grady. Deceptive Diagnosis, Bemidji: Focus, 2006. Print.

Tyler, David. God's Funeral, Bemidji: Focus`, 2009. Print.

Walker, Clarence Earl. Biblical Counseling with African Americans: Taking a Ride in the Ethiopian's Chariot, Grand Rapids: Zondervan, 1992. Print.

Welch, Edward T. Side by Side: Walking with Others in Wisdom and Love, Wheaton: Crossway, 2015. Print.

Whitaker, Scott, and Jose' Fleming. Medisin, Wildomar: Divine Protection Publications, 2007.   Print.

Witt, Rush. A Strategy for Incorporating Biblical Counseling in North American Church Plans,   Phillipsburg: P & R, 2019. Print.

Wood, Garth. The Myth of Neurosis, New York: Harper & Row, 1987. Print.

Wright, H. Norman. The Premarital Counseling Handbook, Chicago: Moody, 1992. Print.

Appendix A

S.O.S.

Survey

Please answer the following questions. Your answers are for research only and your identity will not be revealed.

1. What is your chosen method of counseling?

  ○ Secular Counseling

  ○ Christian Counseling

  ○ Biblical Counseling

  ○ Other (please specify)

  [   ]

2. How long have you been counseling?

  ○ 1-5 years

  ○ 5-10 years

  ○ 10-15 years

  ○ > 15 years

3. What are your counseling credentials?

  ○ Psychologist: Doctorate Level. PhD, PsyD, EdD

  ○ Psychologist: Masters Level. MA, MS, LGPC, LCPC.

  ○ Social Worker. MSW, LGSW, LCSW, LMSW, LCSW-C, LISW, LSW

  ○ Marriage and Family Therapist

  ○ Pastoral Counseling

4. My credentials are adequate for the counseling I do.

  ○ Strongly agree

  ○ Agree

  ○ Neither agree nor disagree

  ○ Disagree

  ○ Strongly disagree

5. What foundation is your counseling based on?

  ○ Modern Psychology

  ○ The Holy Bible

  ○ A combination of The Holy bible and Modern Psychology

  ○ Other (please specify)

  [   ]

6. How do you view the other two counseling methods?

○ Extremely effective   ○ Not so effective

○ Very effective   ○ Not at all effective

○ Somewhat effective

7. How likely are you to consider the other two counseling methods?

○ Very likely   ○ Unlikely

○ Likely   ○ Very unlikely

○ Neither likely nor unlikely

8. How do you define sin and sickness?

○ Sin is a transgression against Devine law; Sickness is the state of being ill.

○ Sin is evil acts, whether of thought or of deed; Sickness is an unhealthy condition of body and mind.

○ Sin is a transgression against Devine law; Sickness is an unhealthy condition of body and mind.

○ Sin is evil acts, whether of thought or of deed; Sickness is the state of being ill.

○ Other (please specify)

[   ]

9. What would you use to define "Alcoholism," "Kleptomania," and "Bipolar Disorder?"

○ The Holy Bible

○ The DSM-5

○ Wikipedia

○ Other (please specify)

[   ]

10. When the Church starts calling "Sin" Sickness," it no longer needs a Savior, it needs a therapist.

○ Strongly agree   ○ Disagree

○ Agree   ○ Strongly disagree

○ Neither agree nor disagree

Sin or Sickness

Appendix B

S.O.S.

Answers

Quiz Summary

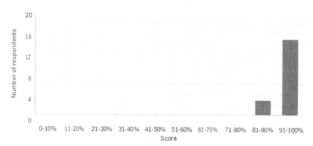

AVERAGE SCORE
98% • 9.8/10 PTS

STATISTICS

Lowest Score	Median	Highest Score
90%	100%	100%

Mean: 98%

Standard Deviation: 4%

Question Ranking

QUESTIONS (10)	DIFFICULTY	AVERAGE SCORE
Q5 What foundation is your counseling based on?	1	94%
Q2 How long have you been counseling?	2	100%
Q6 How do you view the other two counseling methods?	2	100%
Q1 What is your chosen method of counseling?	2	100%
Q7 How likely are you to consider the other two counseling methods?	2	100%
Q3 What are your counseling credentials?	2	100%
Q4 My credentials are adequate for the counseling I do.	2	100%
Q9 What would you use to define "Alcoholism," "Kleptomania," and "Bipolar Disorder?"	2	100%
Q10 When the Church starts calling "Sin" Sickness," it no longer needs a Savior, it needs a therapist.	2	100%
Q8 How do you define sin and sickness?	2	100%

Q1 What is your chosen method of counseling?

Answered 18   Skipped 0

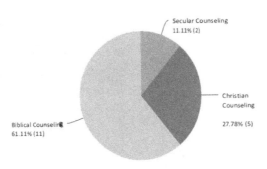

Secular Counseling
11.11% (2)

Christian
Counseling

27.78% (5)

Biblical Counseling
61.11% (11)

QUIZ STATISTICS

Percent Correct 100%	Average Score 1.0/1.0 (100%)	Standard Deviation 0.00	Difficulty 2/10

ANSWER CHOICES	SCORE	RESPONSES	
3 Secular Counseling	1/1	11.11%	2
3 Christian Counseling	1/1	27.78%	5
3 Biblical Counseling	1/1	61.11%	11
Other (please specify)	–	0.00%	0
TOTAL			18

Q2 How long have you been counseling?

Answered: 18   Skipped: 0

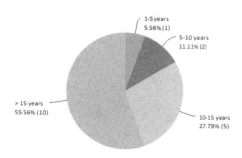

1-5 years
5.56% (1)

5-10 years
11.11% (2)

> 15 years
55.56% (10)

10-15 years
27.78% (5)

QUIZ STATISTICS

Percent Correct 100%	Average Score 1.0/1.0 (100%)	Standard Deviation 0.00	Difficulty 2/10

ANSWER CHOICES	SCORE	RESPONSES	
3 1-5 years	1/1	5.56%	1
3 5-10 years	1/1	11.11%	2
3 10-15 years	1/1	27.78%	5
3 > 15 years	1/1	55.56%	10
TOTAL			**18**

107

Q3 What are your counseling credentials?

Answered: 18   Skipped: 0

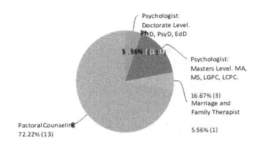

Psychologist:
Doctorate Level.
PhD, PsyD, EdD

5.56% (1)

Psychologist:
Masters Level. MA,
MS, LGPC, LCPC.

16.67% (3)
Marriage and
Family Therapist

5.56% (1)

Pastoral Counseling
72.22% (13)

QUIZ STATISTICS

Percent Correct	Average Score	Standard Deviation	Difficulty
100%	1.0/1.0 (100%)	0.00	2/10

ANSWER CHOICES	SCORE	RESPONSES	
3 Psychologist: Doctorate Level. PhD, PsyD, EdD	1/1	5.56%	1
3 Psychologist: Masters Level. MA, MS, LGPC, LCPC	1/1	16.67%	3
3 Social Worker. MSW, LGSW, LCSW, LMSW, LCSW-C, LISW, LSW	1/1	0.00%	0
3 Marriage and Family Therapist	1/1	5.56%	1
3 Pastoral Counseling	1/1	72.22%	13
TOTAL			18

108

Q4 My credentials are adequate for the counseling I do.

Answered: 18   Skipped: 0

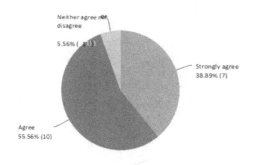

QUIZ STATISTICS

Percent Correct	Average Score	Standard Deviation	Difficulty
100%	1.0/1.0 (100%)	0.00	2/10

ANSWER CHOICES	SCORE	RESPONSES	
3 Strongly agree	1/1	38.89%	7
3 Agree	1/1	55.56%	10
3 Neither agree nor disagree	1/1	5.56%	1
3 Disagree	1/1	0.00%	0
3 Strongly disagree	1/1	0.00%	0
TOTAL			18

Q5 What foundation is your counseling based on?

Answered: 18   Skipped: 0

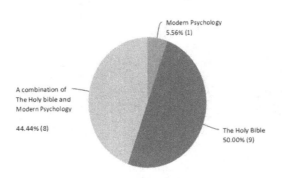

Modern Psychology
5.56% (1)

A combination of
The Holy bible and
Modern Psychology

44.44% (8)

The Holy Bible
50.00% (9)

QUIZ STATISTICS

Percent Correct	Average Score	Standard Deviation	Difficulty
94%	0.9/1.0 (94%)	0.24	1/10

ANSWER CHOICES	SCORE	RESPONSES	
Modern Psychology	0/1	5.56%	1
3 The Holy Bible	1/1	50.00%	9
3 A combination of The Holy bible and Modern Psychology	1/1	44.44%	8
Other (please specify)	–	0.00%	0
TOTAL			**18**

110

Q6 How do you view the other two counseling methods?

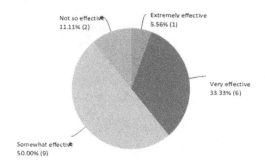

Not so effective
11.11% (2)

Extremely effective
5.56% (1)

Very effective
33.33% (6)

Somewhat effective
50.00% (9)

QUIZ STATISTICS

Percent Correct	Average Score	Standard Deviation	Difficulty
100%	1.0/1.0 (100%)	0.00	2/10

ANSWER CHOICES	SCORE	RESPONSES	
3 Extremely effective	1/1	5.56%	1
3 Very effective	1/1	33.33%	6
3 Somewhat effective	1/1	50.00%	9
3 Not so effective	1/1	11.11%	2
3 Not at all effective	1/1	0.00%	0
TOTAL			18

Q7 How likely are you to consider the other two counseling methods?

Answered: 18   Skipped: 0

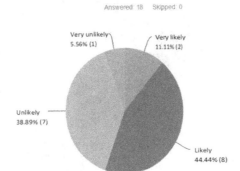

QUIZ STATISTICS

Percent Correct	Average Score	Standard Deviation	Difficulty
100%	1.0/1.0 (100%)	0.00	2/10

ANSWER CHOICES	SCORE	RESPONSES	
3 Very likely	1/1	11.11%	2
3 Likely	1/1	44.44%	8
3 Neither likely nor unlikely	1/1	0.00%	0
3 Unlikely	1/1	38.89%	7
3 Very unlikely	1/1	5.56%	1
TOTAL			18

112

Q8 How do you define sin and sickness?

Answered: 18   Skipped: 0

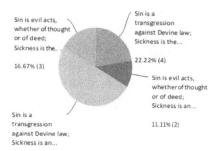

Sin is evil acts, whether of thought or of deed; Sickness is the...

16.67% (3)

Sin is a transgression against Devine law; Sickness is the...

22.22% (4)

Sin is evil acts, whether of thought or of deed; Sickness is an...

11.11% (2)

Sin is a transgression against Devine law; Sickness is an...

QUIZ STATISTICS

Percent Correct	Average Score	Standard Deviation	Difficulty
100%	1.0/1.0 (100%)	0.00	2/10

ANSWER CHOICES	SCORE	RESPONSES	
3 Sin is a transgression against Devine law; Sickness is the state of being ill.	1/1	22.22%	4
3 Sin is evil acts, whether of thought or of deed; Sickness is an unhealthy condition of body and mind.	1/1	11.11%	2
3 Sin is a transgression against Devine law; Sickness is an unhealthy condition of body and mind.	1/1	50.00%	9
3 Sin is evil acts, whether of thought or of deed; Sickness is the state of being ill.	1/1	16.67%	3
Other (please specify)	--	0.00%	0
TOTAL			18

113

Q8 How do you define sin and sickness?

Answered: 18   Skipped: 0

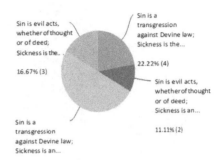

Sin is evil acts, whether of thought or of deed; Sickness is the..

16.67% (3)

Sin is a transgression against Devine law; Sickness is an...

Sin is a transgression against Devine law; Sickness is the...

22.22% (4)

Sin is evil acts, whether of thought or of deed; Sickness is an...

11.11% (2)

QUIZ STATISTICS

Percent Correct	Average Score	Standard Deviation	Difficulty
100%	1.0/1.0 (100%)	0.00	2/10

ANSWER CHOICES	SCORE	RESPONSES	
Sin is a transgression against Devine law; Sickness is the state of being ill.	1/1	22.22%	4
Sin is evil acts, whether of thought or of deed; Sickness is an unhealthy condition of body and mind.	1/1	11.11%	2
Sin is a transgression against Devine law; Sickness is an unhealthy condition of body and mind.	1/1	50.00%	9
Sin is evil acts, whether of thought or of deed; Sickness is the state of being ill	1/1	16.67%	3
Other (please specify)	--	0.00%	0
TOTAL			18

114

Q9 What would you use to define "Alcoholism," "Kleptomania," and "Bipolar Disorder?"

Answered: 17   Skipped: 1

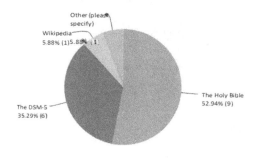

QUIZ STATISTICS

Percent Correct 89%	Average Score 1.0/1.0 (100%)	Standard Deviation 0.00	Difficulty 2/10

ANSWER CHOICES	SCORE	RESPONSES	
⊃ The Holy Bible	1/1	52.94%	9
⊃ The DSM-5	1/1	35.29%	6
⊃ Wikipedia	1/1	5.88%	1
Other (please specify)	–	5.88%	1
TOTAL			17

115

Q10 When the Church starts calling "Sin" Sickness," it no longer needs a Savior, it needs a therapist.

Answered: 18   Skipped: 0

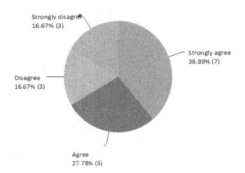

QUIZ STATISTICS

Percent Correct	Average Score	Standard Deviation	Difficulty
100%	1.0/1.0 (100%)	0.00	2/10

ANSWER CHOICES	SCORE	RESPONSES	
3 Strongly agree	1/1	38.89%	7
3 Agree	1/1	27.78%	5
Neither agree nor disagree	0/1	0.00%	0
3 Disagree	1/1	16.67%	3
3 Strongly disagree	1/1	16.67%	3
TOTAL			18

116

ACKNOWLEDGEMENTS

First and foremost, I thank God for allowing me to do this. The Lord is faithful and to Him be the glory.

I want to thank my "good thing," my wife, Surenell, Thank you for all the love and support you've shown while I was completing this.

To the faculty and staff of Master's International University of Divinity, thank you. Your school is a blessing to all who attend.

A very special "Thank you" to Dr. Cheryl Durham. Thank you for teaching me the difference between writing a sermon manuscript and writing a scholarly paper. This is a lesson I will never forget.

To my publisher, Cassandra Oakes, you're the greatest! Thank you for all that you do!

Finally, to the reader: Thank you for taking the time to read this book. May it serve as a beacon of light on a subject that is clouded in darkness. I pray that you will be informed and enlightened. Thank you and may God bless.

To God be the Glory!

A BLESSED WEEK

May your MONDAY be MARVELOUS
As you start out on your week
May your TUESDAY be TERIFFIC
As you find that in which you seek
May your WEDNESDAY be WONDERFUL
As your weekend comes into view
May your THURSDAY be TRIUMPHFANT
As you know just what to do
May your FRIDAY be FANTASTIC
As you just can't wait
May your SATURDAY be SPECTACULAR
As you rest and rejuvenate
May your SUNDAY be SAINTLY
As you give thanks to your Creator
May your week be full
Of HIS Blessings and HIS Favor

by
Dr. Stan McCrary

Dr. Stanley K. McCrary

Dr. McCrary lives in Steens, MS where he is married to his 1st grade sweetheart Surenell and together they have five children: Marie, LaKiesha, Erica, Xavier, Kapri, and two grandchildren: Laila and Jeffery.

Dr. Stanley K McCrary is a 1978 graduate of Pickens County High School of Reform, AL. That same year he joined the United States Navy. While in the Navy he earned an Associate Degree in Computer Science at San Diego Mesa College in San Diego, CA. He retired in 1998 after proudly serving his country for 20 years in the Submarine Service. He worked in Chicago as a Design Engineer and then on to Atlanta as a mid-level manager for the same company, SBC Telecom.

In August on 2001 he answered his calling into the ministry and preached his first sermon on Veteran's Day, November 11, 2001. In May of 2002 he was called to Mt Pleasant Baptist Church and was installed as Pastor in August of that same year.

Following the advice of the Apostle Paul Pastor McCrary continued his studies of God and His Word. He earned his doctorate (Biblical Studies in Theology) from Master's International School of Divinity in Evansville, IN on July 19,

2008. He served as the Dean of Christian Education for the Lebanon Baptist Association for over five years and lectured for five years at the Alabama State Baptist Women's Convention. In September of 2016 he was called to pastor the Friendship Missionary Baptist Church of Columbus, MS. He also serves as the Vice Moderator of the Mt Olivet District Association and teaches in the Northeast Mississippi State Baptist Convention and the Sunday School Congress of Christian Education. Dr. McCrary is the Academic Dean and professor at the Ministerial Institution and College in West Point, MS. In April of 2021, Dr. McCrary graduated from Master's International University of Divinity with his second doctorate degree (Biblical Studies in Biblical Counseling).

Dr. McCrary is a published author and was nominated as Best Inspirational Author at the 2018 Gospel Image Awards for his book, *The Church: Past, Present, and Future.* His second book, *SOS: Sin Or Sickness, the Church Must Decide!* is scheduled to be released this Fall. Dr McCrary is a Distinguished Toastmaster and regularly speaks to civic organizations providing thoughtful insight on a variety of subjects. He is the Past President of the United Way of Lowndes County and is the President of the Columbus Lowndes County Community Chaplains (CLC3), a joint partnership with the Chaplains of Columbus Air Force Base.